The Essential Bu

TRIUM

# TRIDENT

BSA

# ROCKET III

1968 to 1976

Your marque expert:
Chris Rooke

**VELOCE PUBLISHING**
THE PUBLISHER OF FINE AUTOMOTIVE BOOKS

Essential Buyer's Guide Series
Alfa Romeo Alfasud (Metcalfe)
Alfa Romeo Alfetta: all saloon/sedan models 1972 to 1984 & coupé models 1974 to 1987 (Metcalfe)
Alfa Romeo Giulia GT Coupé (Booker)
Alfa Romeo Giulia Spider (Booker & Talbott)
Audi TT (Davies)
Audi TT Mk2 2006 to 2014 (working title) (Durnan)
Austin-Healey Big Healeys (Trummel)
BMW Boxer Twins (Henshaw)
BMW E30 3 Series 1981 to 1994 (Hosier)
BMW GS (Henshaw)
BMW X5 (Saunders)
BMW Z3 Roadster (Fishwick)
BMW Z4: E85 Roadster and E86 Coupé including M and Alpina 2003 to 2009 (Smitheram)
BSA 350, 441 & 500 Singles (Henshaw)
BSA 500 & 650 Twins (Henshaw)
BSA Bantam (Henshaw)
Choosing, Using & Maintaining Your Electric Bicycle (Henshaw)
Citroën 2CV (Paxton)
Citroën ID & DS (Heilig & Heilig)
Cobra Replicas (Ayre)
Corvette C2 Sting Ray 1963-1967 (Falconer)
Datsun 240Z 1969 to 1973 (Newlyn)
DeLorean DMC-12 1981 to 1983 (Williams)
Ducati Bevel Twins (Falloon)
Ducati Desmodue Twins (Falloon)
Ducati Desmoquattro Twins – 851, 888, 916, 996, 998, ST4 1988 to 2004 (Falloon)
Fiat 500 & 600 (Bobbitt)
Ford Capri (Paxton)
Ford Escort Mk1 & Mk2 (Williamson)
Ford Model A – All Models 1927 to 1931 (Buckley & Cobell)
Ford Model T – All models 1909 to 1927 (Barker & Tuckett)
Ford Mustang (Cook)
Ford Mustang – First Generation 1964 to 1973 (Cook)
Ford RS Cosworth Sierra & Escort (Williamson)
Harley-Davidson Big Twins (Henshaw)
Hillman Imp (Morgan)
Hinckley Triumph triples & fours 750, 900, 955, 1000, 1050, 1200 – 1991-2009 (Henshaw)
Honda CBR FireBlade (Henshaw)
Honda CBR600 Hurricane (Henshaw)
Honda SOHC Fours 1969-1984 (Henshaw)
Jaguar E-Type 3.8 & 4.2 litre (Crespin)
Jaguar E-type V12 5.3 litre (Crespin)
Jaguar Mark 1 & 2 (All models including Daimler 2.5-litre V8) 1955 to 1969 (Thorley)
Jaguar New XK 2005-2014 (Thorley)
Jaguar S-Type – 1999 to 2007 (Thorley)
Jaguar X-Type – 2001 to 2009 (Thorley)
Jaguar XJ-S (Crespin)
Jaguar XJ6, XJ8 & XJR (Thorley)
Jaguar XK 120, 140 & 150 (Thorley)
Jaguar XK8 & XKR (1996-2005) (Thorley)
Jaguar/Daimler XJ 1994-2003 (Crespin)
Jaguar/Daimler XJ40 (Crespin)
Jaguar/Daimler XJ6, XJ12 & Sovereign (Crespin)
Kawasaki Z1 & Z900 (Orritt)
Land Rover Discovery Series 1 1989 to 1998 (Taylor)
Land Rover Series I, II & IIA (Thurman)
Land Rover Series III (Thurman)
Lotus Elan – S1, S2, S3, S4 & Sprint 1962 to 1973 – Plus 2, Plus 2S 130/5 1967 to 1974 (Vale)
Lotus Europa – S1, S2, Twin-cam & Special 1966 to 1975 (Vale)
Lotus Seven replicas & Caterham 7: 1973-2013 (Hawkins)
Mazda MX-5 Miata (Mk1 1989-97 & Mk2 98-2001) (Crook)
Mazda RX-8 (Parish)
Mercedes Benz Pagoda 230SL, 250SL & 280SL roadsters & coupés (Bass)
Mercedes-Benz 190: all 190 models (W201 series) 1982 to 1993 (Parish)
Mercedes-Benz 280-560SL & SLC (Bass)
Mercedes-Benz SL R129-series 1989 to 2001 (Parish)
Mercedes-Benz SLK (Bass)
Mercedes-Benz W123 (Parish)
Mercedes-Benz W124 – All models 1984-1997 (Zoporowski)
MG Midget & A-H Sprite (Horler)
MG TD, TF & TF1500 (Jones)
MGA 1955-1962 (Crosier & Sear)
MGB & MGB GT (Williams)
MGF & MG TF (Hawkins)
Mini (Paxton)
Morris Minor & 1000 (Newell)
Moto Guzzi 2-valve big twins (Falloon)
New Mini (Collins)
Norton Commando (Henshaw)
Peugeot 205 GTI (Blackburn)
Piaggio Scooters – all modern two-stroke & four-stroke automatic models 1991 to 2016 (Willis)
Porsche 911 (964) (Streather)
Porsche 911 (993) (Streather)
Porsche 911 (996) (Streather)
Porsche 911 (997) – Model years 2004 to 2009 (Streather)
Porsche 911 (997) – Second generation models 2009 to 2012 (Streather)
Porsche 911 Carrera 3.2 (Streather)
Porsche 911SC (Streather)
Porsche 924 – All models 1976 to 1988 (Hodgkins)
Porsche 928 (Hemmings)
Porsche 930 Turbo & 911 (930) Turbo (Streather)
Porsche 944 (Higgins & Mitchell)
Porsche 981 Boxster & Cayman (Streather)
Porsche 986 Boxster (Streather)
Porsche 987 Boxster & Cayman (first gen) (Streather)
Porsche 987 Boxster & Cayman (second gen) (Streather)
Range Rover – First Generation models 1970 to 1996 (Taylor)
Rolls-Royce Silver Shadow & Bentley T-Series (Bobbitt)
Royal Enfield Bullet (Henshaw)
Subaru Impreza (Hobbs)
Sunbeam Alpine (Barker)
Triumph 350 & 500 Twins (Henshaw)
Triumph Bonneville (Henshaw)
Triumph Stag (Mort & Fox)
Triumph Thunderbird, Trophy & Tiger (Henshaw)
Triumph TR2, & TR3 – All models (including 3A & 3B) 1953 to 1962 (Conners)
Triumph TR6 (Williams)
Triumph TR7 & TR8 (Williams)
TVR S-series – S1, S2, S3/S3C, S4C & V8S 1986 to 1994 (Kitchen)
Velocette 350 & 500 Singles 1946 to 1970 (Henshaw)
Vespa Scooters – Classic two-stroke models 1960-2008 (Paxton)
Volkswagen Bus (Copping & Cservenka)
Volvo 700/900 Series (Beavis)
Volvo P1800/1800S, E & ES 1961 to 1973 (Murray)
VW Beetle (Copping & Cservenka)
VW Golf GTI (Copping & Cservenka)

# www.veloce.co.uk

First published in October 2018 by Veloce Publishing Limited, Veloce House, Parkway Farm Business Park, Middle Farm Way, Poundbury, Dorchester, Dorset, DT1 3AR, England.
Telephone 01305 260068/Fax 01305 250479/email info@veloce.co.uk/web www.veloce.co.uk or www.velocebooks.com.
ISBN: 978-1-787113-80-0 UPC: 6-36847-01380-6

British Library Cataloguing in Publication Data – A catalogue record for this book is available from the British Library.
Typesetting, design and page make-up all by Veloce Publishing Ltd on Apple Mac.
Printed and bound in India by Replika Press.

# Introduction
– the purpose of this book

The Triumph Trident and BSA Rocket III are iconic, classic machines in the pantheon of British motorcycles. With wonderful three-cylinder engines (as opposed to the usual twins of the era), and, despite a rather luke-warm reception on their original release, they sold successfully at the time, and are now becoming ever increasingly sought-after and admired as a classic motorcycle.

Triumph and BSA realised that their twin cylinder motorcycles couldn't really be made to work above 650cc due to problems with engine vibration on the 180-degree crankshafts. Norton tried to overcome this problem with its Isolastic engine mounting system (basically the engine was mounted on rubber bushes), and, driven by a necessity to keep up with its competitors, Triumph did eventually go on to produce a 750cc Bonneville. However, the Triple's 120-degree crankshaft meant less vibration and an engine that thrived on revs and went like stink. Probably the most famous Triple of all is 'Slippery Sam,' which won the Isle of Man Production TT five times in a row in the early '70s. The combination of speed and handling required to achieve this amazing feat says it all. Meanwhile, not to be outdone, BSA also set several new speed records on a standard Rocket III.

This book is a practical guide to buying a secondhand machine, and gives advice on what to look for to ensure you buy a good bike and avoid a complete lemon – and there are many out there. This book isn't an originality guide, so you won't find full details of every minute change made to the bikes during their production run. Such information is available elsewhere for those who require it. What you will find is a general guide to the different models produced, their year-by-year specification changes, and what to look for when viewing a Triple.

As early as 1963, the legendary designers Doug Hele and Burt Hopwood were looking for an alternative to their range of twin-engined machines, and considered building a Triple. Unfortunately, due mainly to the state of the industry at the time, the bikes weren't launched until autumn 1968, just as Honda launched its CB750-4, which rather eclipsed the Triple.

The advantage that the Triples had over the Honda was that they were fast and handled well. Where they lost out to the Honda was in having no electric start, quality control problems, no disc brakes, a four-speed gearbox, and, despite famous design studio Ogle having designed the tank and side panels, slightly odd-looking styling. Triumph and BSA spent the next few years playing catch-up with the Honda, slowly adding a disc brake to the front and a five-speed gearbox, as well as introducing a 'Beauty Kit' for export models to replace the much-despised Ogle tank and panels, especially in the all-important American market, and producing such exotic models as the Hurricane X-75.

However, it wasn't until 1975 that Triumph finally unveiled the ultimate Triple: the T160, with forward slanting cylinders, disc brakes all-round, a five-speed gearbox with left-foot change and (gasp) an electric starter! The T160 combined the speed and handling of the earlier bikes with the usability and style of the Honda. But it was too little, too late, and, after a year, Triumph folded and the Triple was no more. Over the years there were just over 33,000 Triples built.

Today they are much revered as a real thoroughbred of a bike, with an engine that howls above 5000 revs, and with handling that match their power. It's really at

The famous five-time Isle of Man Production TT winner, 'Slippery Sam.'

home on 'A' roads, and is a machine that brings a wide smile to the face of all who ride them. A classic British bike with racing pedigree, which is a joy to own and ride.

There are many people who have helped with the publication of this book and whom I would like to thank. First of all my thanks go to the people of the Trident and Rocket III Owners' Club (TR3OC) for their knowledge, expertise and enthusiasm. Thanks also to parts suppliers such as LP Williams who are very helpful and knowledgeable and help to keep Triples on the road. Also thanks to the following for contributing their thoughts, expertise and photos: Piet Adriaans, Chris Bashall, Chris Birkett, Clive Blake, Peter Charlton, Cliffe Clayton, Richard Davies, David Drew, Gary Heap, Roy Kilgour, Steve Lakin, Peter Lord, Miller Malcolm, Bernie McCann, Vince Newman, Martin Rawson, Graham Small, Tim Riley, Chris Wellwood, Gary Westwater, John Young and Costa Zafiri.

A lovely MkII Rocket III.

# Contents

**Introduction**
– the purpose of this book.. .. .. .. .. 3

**1 Is it the right bike for you?**
– marriage guidance .. .. .. .. .. .. .. 6

**2 Cost considerations**
– affordable, or a money pit? .. .. .. .. 8

**3 Living with a Trident/Rocket**
– will you get along together? . .. .. .. 9

**4 Relative values**
– which model for you? .. .. .. .. .. .12

**5 Before you view**
– be well informed .. .. .. .. .. .. .. .18

**6 Inspection equipment**
– these items will really help .. .. .. .21

**7 Fifteen minute evaluation**
– walk away or stay? .. .. .. .. .. .. .22

**8 Key points**
– where to look for problems .. .. .. .25

**9 Serious evaluation**
– 30 minutes for years of enjoyment .26

**10 Auctions**
– sold! Another way to buy your
dream. .. .. .. .. .. .. .. .. .. .. .44

**11 Paperwork**
– correct documentation is essential!.. 46

**12 What's it worth?**
– let your head rule your heart .. .. .48

**13 Do you really want to
restore?**
– it'll take longer and cost more
than you think. .. .. .. .. .. .. .. .. .49

**14 Paint problems**
– bad complexion, including dimples,
pimples and bubbles .. .. .. .. .. .. .51

**15 Problems due to lack of use**
– just like their owners,
Tridents/Rockets need exercise .. .. .53

**16 The Community**
– key people, organisations and
companies in the Trident/Rocket
world.. .. .. .. .. .. .. .. .. .. .. .55

**17 Vital statistics**
– essential data at your fingertips .. .58

**Index** .. .. .. .. .. .. .. .. .. .. .64

---

**THE ESSENTIAL BUYER'S GUIDE™ CURRENCY**
At the time of publication a BG unit of currency "●" equals approximately
£1.00/US$1.32/Euro 1.13. Please adjust to suit current exchange rates using
Sterling as the base currency.

# 1 Is it the right bike for you?
– marriage guidance

## Tall and short riders
Triples are relatively heavy bikes and quite tall, so not that easy to move around the garage or at low speeds. Seat heights are 30-32in, and both T150s and Rocket IIIs weigh around 470lb, with the T160 even heavier at 552lb.

## Running costs
Triples aren't renowned for being frugal when it comes to petrol consumption, and spares can be expensive, but all Triples now qualify as Vehicles of Historic Interest (VHI) in the UK, with no requirement for an annual MoT, and no road tax to pay.

## Maintenance
Don't forget that, as with any classic machine, Triples require regular maintenance and aren't like modern 'ride it and forget it' machines. Regular oil changes, tappet, rear chain/primary chain and clutch adjustment are essential to keep these machines running properly.

## Starting
All Triples have kickstarts fitted, and the T160 also has electric start which works well, especially with modern batteries, electronic ignition and mainly summer use. Kickstarting is relatively easy compared to a big British twin. Electric starter conversions are also now available for earlier models, either as kits or fully fitted.

## Usability
Triples are definitely not around-town commuter bikes. Apart from their weight, they have quite heavy clutches, and don't like sitting in traffic. The open road, especially faster 'A' roads, is where they come into their own, and prove they are highly capable machines. Many Triples were, and still are, used on the race track. They can make decent touring bikes, but they are very thirsty.

## Parts availability
Parts availability is excellent and improving all the time, as parts specialists continue to make previously unavailable parts available. Even crankcases are now being manufactured. However, there are parts that are currently NLA (no longer available), and these are listed in chapter 4.

## Parts costs
Parts aren't the cheapest, and a full engine rebuild costs considerably more than a twin (there's more of it and it's a bit more complicated), but parts are generally of high quality, and many upgrades are available.

## Insurance
Insurance isn't any higher than for a comparable machine. Brokers such as Carole Nash and Footman James offer good classic policies, but it's always worth researching to find the best policy for you.

## Investment potential

Just over 30,000 Triples were produced, and original examples are all very good investments, with Rocket IIIs and T160s offering particularly good returns. The best investment of all is probably the Hurricane X-75, which continues to demand exceptionally high prices.

Immaculate modified T150.

Triples are beautiful machines in every respect – here's a T160 in custom colours.

Triumph Hurricane X-75.

### Foibles

The Triple's clutch is a single dry plate rather than the more normal wet multi-plate version used in twins; it can be very hard to set up and is quite heavy to operate. Bikes can pull slightly to the left as the engine is offset $\frac{5}{32}$in from centre, to help the rear chain avoid the rear tyre.

### Plus points

A real racing thoroughbred that is very fast and handles well. It thrives on revs, and many enthusiasts will tell you that there's nothing like the howl of a Triple on full song.

### Minus points

Needs regular/constant maintenance, and is rather heavy and awkward at low speeds. Triples also have a tendency to burn oil (signalled by blue smoke from the exhaust), which can be hard to cure. Triples are also renowned for breaking conrods which then exit the crankcases at high speed – not good! Many owners fit steel or billet alloy conrods during an engine rebuild to avoid this possibility. A bit more difficult to maintain than a twin.

### Alternatives

Other triples are available, most notably the Laverda Jota, which is faster, but probably has even more foibles than a Triple! Others to consider include the Kawasaki H2 750 two-stroke (for the brave/insane) and the Yamaha XS750 (shaft drive).

# 2 Cost considerations
– affordable, or a money pit?

The spares situation for Triples is excellent. Virtually every part is available, including crankcases, and only a few parts are currently NLA (no longer available). There are several specialist suppliers who are very knowledgeable, and their range of spares continues to expand. The range of upgraded parts is also increasing for those who wish to fit more modern technology, such as brakes, electrics, and ignition and fuel systems.

Drilled brake discs are now available.

Complete restoration cost from basket case to concours is expensive at around ●x10,000, depending on upgrades etc.

Example parts prices:
Front brake master cylinder ●x135
Carburettor ●x122 (each)
Piston and rings ●x93 (each)
Valve guide ●x13 (each)
Valves ●x15 (each)
Big end shells ●x40 (set)
Main bearing shells ●x35 (set)
Oil pump (complete) ●x220
Timing cover ●x230
Raygun exhaust silencers ●x145 (each)
Hurricane silencer set ●x295
T160 silencer ●x116 (each)
T150 3-into-1 exhaust system ●x785
Standard brake disc ●x45
Drilled brake disc ●x59
Rocket III wiring harness ●x90
T160 braided wiring harness ●x129
Tri-spark electronic ignition ●x220
Boyer electronic ignition ●x110
T150 rear mudguard ●x185
T160 rear mudguard ●x154
Twin-disc conversion ●x630-780
Front fork stanchion ●x57
Rear shock absorbers ●x128 (pair)
T160 headlamp shell and rim ●x110
Re-con rocker box ●x145 (complete)

Twin-disc upgrade fitted to a T160.

Virtually all engine and gearbox parts are available.

Wiring harnesses are available.

# 3 Living with a Trident/Rocket III

– will you get along together?

To be honest, if you've never owned a classic bike then you might want to think twice before buying a Triple. These are high maintenance machines, thoroughbreds that are very rewarding to ride, but need constant fettling to keep them in top condition. As with most classics, they're not like a modern 'ride it and forget it' bike, and they're not good for commuting or riding across town or on rough roads. However, if you've some experience with classic bikes and are relatively mechanically-minded, then a Triple is a must for any British bike enthusiast.

Apart from the T160, you'll need to kickstart them – although once you get the knack this isn't too hard. You

A great selection of bikes at the annual 'Beezumph' Rally.

Beezumph attracts many Triple enthusiasts.

may also discover that the earlier drum brakes were pretty average by contemporary standards, and downright dreadful by modern ones! Disc brakes on later machines were better – but not by much!

Clutches can be heavy to operate and can drag – badly! Once set up properly they work well, but the amount of work required to achieve this varies enormously from bike-to-bike. On some machines it might just be something simple like needing a new clutch cable, others might require a complete strip down and even the re-machining of parts to get right.

**Lovely original '72 T150.**

Triples have a tendency to burn oil and send a plume of blue smoke out of the exhausts – especially when hot (see page 37 for more on this). The smoke tends to come not from worn valve guides, but from the cylinder bores. It is unclear why Triples sometimes smoke so much, but it's linked primarily to poor machining tolerances and poor quality piston rings. However, some Triples never burn any oil, whereas others do despite having had their engines carefully rebuilt.

That said, part of the joy of owning such an iconic classic as a Triple is tinkering with it and fettling it. Many current owners no longer ride these bikes as everyday transport, but own them as second or third bikes, and only use them in the summer. Thus many owners enjoy working on their bikes in the winter, so minimal work is required in the warmer months.

There are also many modern upgrades available to make riding a Triple an altogether more enjoyable and user-friendly experience. Back in the day, when owners tended to be younger, we all accepted the foibles of such machines, and got on with it. These days as the average age of riders has increased and motor vehicle technology has improved almost beyond belief, riders are more demanding. This is where the various available upgrades come into play.

There are twin-disc brake upgrades with floating callipers and drilled discs; electronic ignition; various clutch upgrades; electric start (all Triples can now be converted to electric start courtesy of such items as a Dave Madigan starter conversion – and these work very well); improved suspension units; uprated electrics; a variety of improved carburettors; sports exhaust systems ... the list goes on. Such upgrades can make Triple ownership very satisfying.

There is also a very good support network for Triples. The excellent owners' club the TR3OC (Trident and Rocket III Owners' Club), is very active, and holds its annual 'Beezumph' rally at a racetrack each year, where owners can ride their mounts round the track if they wish (there are different classes to suit rider experience), or sit back and watch some of the racing specials go round at amazing speeds. There are also many publications to help owners keep their bikes on the road, some produced by the TR3OC, and others, such as the *Haynes Manual*

**Triples aren't just racers – a Rocket III fitted with an electric start conversion, ready to travel.**

and the original *Triumph Workshop Manual,* are still widely available. I should also mention the excellent *Triumph Trident and Rocket III Restoration Manual* – written by yours truly and published by Veloce, aimed at those new to Triples ownership who want to learn more about maintaining their bikes.

But will you actually enjoy riding a Triple? The Triple is not a commuter or cross-town bike, and certainly not designed to go off-road! Where it excels is on the open road, where its speed and handling are legendary. Don't forget that the famous T150 Trident 'Slippery Sam' won the Isle of Man Production TT five years in a row in the early seventies, which says it all. A Triple can be quite docile at low revs and is fairly well mannered, but take it above 5000 revs and it turns into an out-and-out racer that cries out to be ridden hard. I think it is the unmistakable thrilling howl of a Triple engine at full revs that really sets it apart from such bikes as the twin engine Triumph Bonneville or Norton Commando, which have more of a low-down growl.

Triples were (somewhat incredibly) first marketed as touring bikes whilst Norton Commandos were sold as sports bikes. There are owners who rack up thousands of miles on Triples, crossing continents with ease, but they are first and foremost speed machines. Not only this, but fuel consumption is definitely more akin to a racing superbike than a grand tourer (the first time I rode a Triple I nearly ran out of fuel, as I couldn't believe how much it used!). Most Triples achieve around 35mpg depending on how they're ridden.

In short, the Trident/Rocket III is an iconic classic British motorcycle that is admired wherever it goes, and has the looks and style to match its handling and speed. It's a great motorcycle, but as a real thoroughbred classic, it is equally demanding of regular maintenance and fettling. Buy one and you'll find out what all the fuss is about.

# 4 Relative values
– which model for you?

The Trident/Rocket III was launched in September 1968 to an expectant world, eager for the new model. The bikes boasted a three-cylinder in-line OHV engine with four-speed gearbox, twin leading shoe front brake, an oil cooler (which remained on all models), and triple carburettors. Another unique feature of the triple was its single-plate dry clutch (mostly seen in cars), rather than the more traditional multi-plate wet clutch used in most motorcycles of the era.

The Triples were initially quite well received, but only a short while later, in spring 1969, the Honda CB750 was launched with its four cylinders, SOHC (Single Overhead Camshaft), electric start, five gears, front disc brake, no oil leaks and no requirement to tickle the carbs (!). The Triples were immediately outdated, and the writing was on the wall for them and the British motorcycle industry in general. Having said that, Triples sold steadily throughout their production run, with just over 30,000 bikes produced between 1968 and 1976.

There are several different models of Trident/Rocket III, and despite all sharing the same basic Triple engine, each has its own unique features and style, and some may be more suited to your requirements than others.

Within the three basic models – the Triumph Trident T150, the BSA Rocket III and the Triumph Trident T160 – are a considerable number of models and variants, as Triumph/BSA introduced modifications, such as a five-speed gearbox and disc brakes, as well as introducing American spec models during the eight years of production. Their values are shown here as a relative percentage of the T150.

Another category altogether are the production racers. Both Triumph and BSA used the Triple extensively in their racing programmes, so Triples have a great racing heritage, and therefore production racers are highly valued and sought-after.

## Range availability
### Triumph Trident T150
Triumph Trident T150 1968-1969 Colours: Aquamarine. Raygun silencers, four-speed gearbox with right-foot gear change, telescopic front forks with gaiters, twin leading shoe front brake, triple Amal carburettors.
**100%**
Triumph Trident T150 1970
Colours: Olympic flame/silver tanks with black mudguards and side panels. Beauty Kit models were now available in the USA.*
Triumph Trident T150 1971
Colours: Spring gold and black, black side panels and chrome mudguards. Indicators were fitted, together with cast alloy switchgear, Ceriani front forks fitted with alloy fork legs and without gaiters, conical hubs with a new twin leading shoe (TLS) front

An almost entirely original early T150.

American spec '73 T150V, with three-into-one exhaust.

brake and megaphone silencers. American spec bikes were now available with a traditionally styled tank. A five-speed gearbox was offered as an option.

Triumph Trident T150V 1972
Colours: Regal purple. A five-speed gearbox was now standard. **120%**

Triumph Trident T150V 1973
Colours: Black and red. Reverse cone silencers fitted – colloquially known as cigar silencers, front disc brake.

Triumph Trident T150V 1974
Colours: Black and sundance yellow.
    Just over 19,000 T150s were produced.

  * The Beauty Kit comprised more traditionally styled items, more in keeping with Triumph styling: a teardrop tank, different seat, new exhaust downpipes and silencers, side panels and mudguards. **110%**

**A very original '70 T150 Beauty Kit model – minus side panel transfers.**

## BSA Rocket III
BSA Rocket III MkI 1968-70
Colours: Flamboyant red or Flamboyant blue. Raygun silencers, a duplex cradle frame, cylinders slanted 15 degrees forward, right-foot gear change, TLS front brake, telescopic front forks with gaiters, triple carburettors. **150%**

BSA Rocket III MkII 1971
Colours: Flamboyant red or blue, or Firecracker red, frame painted grey. An export tank was now offered which included chrome panels. Ceriani forks fitted with alloy fork legs and without gaiters together with conical wheel hubs incorporating a new TLS front brake, indicators fitted along with new moulded alloy switchgear, megaphone silencers. A five-speed gearbox was offered as an option. **160%**

**BSA Rocket III racing special.**

BSA Rocket III 1972
Colours: Burgundy with a black frame. Some bikes produced with 5-speed gearboxes.

    Just under 6000 Rocket IIIs were produced.

**Beautiful MkI Rocket III.**

## Triumph Trident T160
Triumph Trident T160 1975
Colours: White with sunflower (yellow) flash, Cherokee red with white flash. Cylinders canted forward as for the Rocket III, front/rear disc brakes, electric start, four-into-two exhaust with upswept annular discharge silencers, left-foot change five-speed gearbox, instrument binnacle (with neutral indicator). Traditional Triumph styling. **160%**[**]

    Just over 7000 T160 models were produced.

**Fantastic BSA Rocket III-based Hyde Harrier.**

**Superb '71 MkII Rocket III.**

**The last of the line, the majestic T160.**

## Triumph Hurricane X-75
Triumph Hurricane X-75 1973
A custom version of the Rocket III with one-piece sculpted tank and seat unit, triple-stacked silencers, larger finned cylinder heads, smaller and fatter rear wheel and extended forks and yokes (and some other detail changes). Colour: Aztec red with yellow stripes. **300%**

Just over 1000 Hurricane models were produced.

There were also some specials and racing machines produced in limited numbers – see the end of this section.

## How they compare
### The Triumph Trident T150
For many, this is the purest form of the Trident, with upright cylinders, a front hub brake, Raygun silencers and a 'breadbin' fuel tank. Triumph and BSA were trying to look to the future with the Trident (although it was only supposed to be a stop-gap model before the wonderful new engine they envisaged for their superbikes was created – needless to say, this never materialised, and the Trident remained as their flagship model). To this end, they decided a restyle was in order to bring the Triumph/BSA marques into the late '60s, ready to take on the '70s. They therefore engaged the Ogle design company to come up with a bike that embraced this new 'space age.' Ogle was famous for such designs as the Bond bug and the Raleigh Chopper, and was seen as a forward-looking company that would create a bike for the future.

As a result of Ogle's intervention, the Trident was launched with Raygun silencers and an oblong tank. The silencers looked like they came out of a Dan Dare comic strip, and the petrol tank, instead of looking futuristic, looked very mundane and was instantly nicknamed the 'bread-bin' by those who failed to see its artistic merit (that's most bikers of the time, and especially American riders).

However, time has passed and the original T150 is now viewed with affection by many, and the petrol tank that was once so derided has become an icon, preferred by many enthusiasts to the later, more conventional tanks. The slightly comic book Raygun silencers were also found to be the most effective silencers of all the Triple models in terms of performance, and are again more appreciated and valued today (and frequently used on racing Triples).

As production continued, so improvements and modifications were made, with

The limited production T160-based Legend.

such changes as the introduction of the Beauty Kit models and subsequent availability of American spec models. There were also changes to the front forks and wheel hubs, silencers, and the addition of indicators and new switchgear, a disc front brake and a five-speed gearbox (in the T150V, with the V being the Roman numeral for five), all making the T150 a more user-friendly machine. So, there are a range of bikes to choose from.

**Weight** 468lb. Seat height 31in.

**Strengths/weaknesses** The earlier models had brakes that were only just adequate for the bike's power, especially the first generation of TLS, and the Ogle styling is either loved or hated; more loved as the years go by. Early models also suffered from a host of basic faults – crankcases and crankshafts to name but two – although any such faults will by now have been addressed. Straight line speed and excellent handling are two big plus points.

**Unavailable parts** Side panels are currently NLA (no longer available) for some early models, as are the early steel lower fork legs and 'breadbin' tank straps.*** Conical wheel hubs are not available for later models. Later moulded alloy switchgear is currently unavailable (although the slightly different LF Harris switch gear from a T140 will act as a replacement on the right-hand side).

## The BSA Rocket III
Perhaps even more singular than the T150 was the Rocket III. It was very similar to the T150, with the following exceptions: different side panels and a covered oil cooler, a duplex cradle frame (unlike Triumph's single down-tube frame), a different gearbox cover, and engine cylinders slanted 15 degrees forward, giving the whole bike a sportier look (Triumph later adopted this design feature for the T160).

Apart from the above, it was essentially the same bike as the Triumph, just perhaps even quirkier in the looks department. They are adored by those who like such things, and are that bit rarer than the Triumph, especially as production finished in 1972. As with the Triumph models, American spec bikes with more traditional tear-drop tanks were also available from 1971. Some later bikes also had five-speed gearboxes and these are highly sought-after.

**Weight** 470lb. Seat height 32in.

**Strengths/weaknesses** The Rocket III has even more radical styling than the T150, which together with its lower production numbers makes it a relatively rare machine. MkIIs are highly sought-after (even the Dove grey frames, allegedly designed to look like nickel-plated Egli frames, and much reviled at the time, are now much more popular). These bikes have a strong following, especially amongst BSA lovers.

**Unavailable parts** Side panels and tank straps are currently NLA for early models,*** as are the steel lower fork legs. Conical wheel hubs are NLA for later models, as is the later moulded alloy switchgear.

## Triumph Hurricane X-75
In the early 1970s, BSA had the foresight to realise there was a demand for a more

traditionally styled custom machine, and engaged the American motorcycle stylist Craig Vetter (of Windjammer fairing fame) to design one based on the Rocket III. This he duly did, and after many problems were overcome (especially excessive noise

from the silencers), the X-75 (based on the Rocket III, which is an A75) was ready to be launched ... just as BSA collapsed. Triumph duly took over the project, and without the slightest blush re-badged the bike as a Triumph, and the Triumph Hurricane X-75 was born.

The styling was a masterclass in design, and the combined tank/seat unit was stunning. The bike also featured an amazing triple-stacked silencer system, and a cylinder head with wider fins to give the engine some attitude. However, on its release the public didn't want to know, and Triumph found the bikes very hard to sell! Not only that, but it found it very difficult to get the bikes to conform to stricter noise legislation in the States. As a result, only just over 1000 were built – but now everyone wants one, and their rarity has pushed prices to dizzying heights in recent years. Prices have increased rapidly in the last few years, and continue to rise.

**The stunning Hurricane X-75.**

**Weight** 444lb. Seat height 31in.

**Strengths/weaknesses** That sculpted seat and tank unit may look divine, but the petrol tank holds only slightly more than 2 gallons, which due to the Triple's heavy thirst can make long distance rides rather stressful! However, many owners buy them for the looks, short blasts, and sheer 'wow!' factor, so everything else is secondary.

**Unavailable parts** Many of the custom parts for the Hurricane are hard to obtain, like the combined seat and tank unit (although at the time of writing these are still available) and the cylinder head, but parts such as new exhausts are easier to source. Conical wheel hubs are also NLA.

## The Triumph Trident T160

In 1975, Triumph released the much improved and modernised Triumph Trident T160 in an effort to keep-up with the competition. The bike featured electric start, disc brakes all-round, traditional styling, an engine with cylinders canted forward 15 degrees à la Rocket III, and a left-foot gear change. In fact, the bike boasted over 200 changes from the T150V it replaced. It was, and still is, a beautiful machine, building on the lines of the Hurricane X-75 – but at the time it was too little, too late (Consider that the Kawasaki Z1 had been introduced in 1972, some 3 years earlier, boasting a four-cylinder horizontally split 900cc engine with DOHC (Double Overhead camshaft), electric start, five gears with left foot change, and front disc brake) and the bikes were made for only one year before NVT collapsed and production ceased.

**Weight** 552lb. Seat height 30in.

**Strengths/weaknesses** In many people's eyes this is the most stylish of all the Triples, with traditional styling, sloping cylinders, upswept silencers and a lovely swooping line to the tank and seat. It also boasted electric start, disc brakes all round, and a five-speed left-foot change gearbox. It is probably the most user-friendly of all the Triples despite its considerable weight. But as a result, prices remain considerably higher than those of the T150 and Rocket III. It was sold with two different size tanks: the larger 4-gallon tank, or the smaller 3-gallon version for the American market.

**Unavailable parts** The right-hand moulded switchgear unique to T160s is unavailable, but right-hand switches with a front brake master cylinder for a Bonneville from LF Harris will fit. The special one-off duplex primary chain for these bikes is unobtainable, and when the originals wear excessively then the only options are to convert to belt drive or fit a triplex chain conversion.

## Racing Triples
Tridents and Rocket IIIs were raced extensively in the early 1970s and they were very successful, especially in the Isle of Man TT where 'Slippery Sam' won five consecutive TT production races from 1971-1975. As a result there are still many racing Triples around today and they have a strong following. They generally have Rob North frames and either a Trident T150 or BSA Rocket III engine. **(200%+ depending on history)**

## Specials
Due to the racing success of the Trident/Rocket III several 'specials' were produced, in particular the Legend (**170%**), the Hyde Harrier (**200%**), and Slippery Sam replicas. Les Williams, the great Triumph technical and tuning guru built nearly 30 Slippery Sam replicas for the road. He then went on to create the 'Legend,' based on the T160 but with slightly different styling and carefully built engines by Jack Shemans. 60 bikes were built, each with its own plaque on the top yoke. Finally there is the Hyde Harrier, developed by the well-known and respected Triumph development engineer, Norman Hyde using Harris frames. These are not only very well engineered bikes with great handling and brakes, but they also look stunning. Kits for the Harrier can still be ordered from Norman Hyde – at a price!

**Strengths/weaknesses:** Some specials were made for track use only, and may not be road legal. Most won't take a pillion, but they're all special by their very nature. Their main problem is that their values tend to vary from high to astronomic for some of the genuine race machines. The other problem is ensuring the provenance of any historic racer.

**Unavailable parts:** As these are specials, engine parts etc are available as for the production bikes, but much of the rest is unique or bespoke.

*\*\*Another version of the Triumph Trident T160 was the Cardinal. Between 20 and 130 bikes (experts differ on this) originally destined for the Saudi Arabian police force, but never shipped, were sold as Cardinals. These were in police spec (screen,*

*panniers, single seat, radio consul, air horns, and crash bars) and painted white. (Quite a few bikes that had already been sold to Saudi Arabia were later repatriated to Europe, and also sold as Cardinals or versions thereof – hence the confusion over the number of Cardinals sold.)*

*\*\*\* Stop Press! I have just learned that stainless steel tank straps are now being re-manufactured by Clive Scarfe – contact details in the rear of this book.*

**The wonderful Hyde Harrier.**

# 5 Before you view
– be well informed

To avoid a wasted journey, and the disappointment of finding that the bike does not match your expectations, it will help if you're very clear about what questions you want to ask before you pick up the telephone. Some of these points might appear basic but when you're excited about the prospect of buying your dream classic, it's amazing how some of the most obvious things slip the mind ... Also check the current values of the model you are interested in, using classic bike magazines which give both a price guide and auction results, as well as on auction web sites such as eBay.

## Where is the bike?
Is it going to be worth travelling a very long way? A locally advertised bike, although it may not sound very interesting, can add to your knowledge for very little effort, so make a visit – it might even be in better condition than expected.

## Dealer or private sale
Establish early on if the bike is being sold by its owner or by a trader. A private owner should have all the history, so don't be afraid to ask detailed questions. A dealer may have more limited knowledge of a bike's history, but should have some documentation. A dealer may offer a warranty/guarantee (ask for a printed copy) and finance.

## Cost of collection and delivery
A dealer may well be used to quoting for delivery. A private owner may agree to meet you halfway, but only agree to this after you have seen the bike at the vendor's address to validate the documents. Conversely, you could meet halfway and agree the sale, but insist on meeting at the vendor's address for the handover.

## View – when and where
It is always preferable to view at the vendor's home or business premises. In the case of a private sale, the bike's documentation should tally with the vendor's name and address. Arrange to view only in daylight and avoid a wet day – the vendor may not let you take the bike for a test ride if it's wet.

## Reason for sale
Do make it one of the first questions. Why is the bike being sold and how long has it been with the current owner? How many previous owners? How original is it and is it an import (if being sold in the UK).

## Condition (engine, paintwork, chrome, wheels)
Ask for an honest appraisal of the bike's condition. Ask specifically about some of the check items described in chapter 8. Also check that all parts of the bike are there, and if not, what is missing? Remember that some parts are unavailable. I always ask the question: 'What work needs doing to it?' or similar. If the owner says 'Nothing,' then he's either not too honest, or he doesn't know the bike that well. Triples generally need something doing to them, however minor, and an honest

seller will give an honest answer to this question. This question should give you important information about the seller and the bike.

## All original specification
A completely original Trident or Rocket III will be worth more than a non-original one, but those with proper upgrades (eg upgraded brakes, electric start, big-bore conversion etc) can also be worth more.

Ask the vendor what upgrades the bike has (if any), and what repair/maintenance work has been carried out.

## Matching data/legal ownership
Do frame, engine numbers and number plate match the official registration document? Is the owner's name and address recorded in the official registration documents?

For those countries that require an annual test of roadworthiness, does the bike have a document showing it complies? (In the UK all Tridents and Rocket IIIs are now classed as Vehicles of Historic Interest, and therefore do not require an MoT test, and road tax is nil).

Does the vendor own the bike outright? Money might be owed to a finance company or bank: the bike could even be stolen. Several organisations will supply the data on ownership, based on the bike's number plate number, for a fee. Such companies can often also tell you whether the bike has been 'written off' by an insurance company. In the UK these organisations can supply vehicle data:

HPI – 01722 422 422 www.hpicheck.com
AA – 0870 600 0836  www.theaa.com
DVLA – 0870 240 0010 www.gov.uk
RAC – 0870 533 3660 www.rac.co.uk

Other countries have similar organisations.

## Unleaded fuel
All Triples run on unleaded fuel without modification.

## Insurance
Check with your existing insurer before setting out, your current policy might not cover you to ride the bike if you do purchase it and want to ride it home.

## How you can pay
A cheque will take several days to clear and the seller may prefer to sell to a cash buyer. However, a banker's draft (a cheque issued by a bank) is a good as cash, but safer. Alternatively you can pay by BACS (electronic money transfer), which these days is instant if you have the app. on your mobile phone

## Buying at auction?
If the intention is to buy at auction, see chapter 10 for further advice.

## Buying from eBay
Many bikes are for sale on online auction sites these days. The first thing to note

is that photos can be very misleading. A general photo of a bike in poor condition looks much the same as a bike in concours condition. If at all possible ask for close-up pictures if they are not already displayed, especially showing any damage or rust or other defects. If you are still interested, arrange to see the bike in person.

## Professional vehicle check (mechanical examination)
There are often marque/model specialists who will undertake professional examination of a vehicle on your behalf. Owners' clubs such as the TR3OC will be able to put you in touch with such specialists.

# 6 Inspection equipment
– these items will really help

**This book**
**Reading glasses (if you need them for close work)**
**Torch**
**Overalls**
**Digital camera**
**Compression tester**
**A friend, preferably a knowledgeable enthusiast**

Before you rush out of the door, gather together a few items that will help as you work your way around the bike. This book is designed to be your guide at every step, so take it along and use the check boxes in chapter 9 to help you assess each area of the bike you're interested in. Don't be afraid to let the seller see you using it.

Take your reading glasses if you need them to read documents and make close up inspections.

A small torch can be useful for looking into some of the harder to see parts.

Be prepared to get dirty. Take along a pair of overalls, if you have them.

If you have the use of a digital camera, take it along so that later you can study some areas of the bike more closely. Take a picture of any part of the bike that causes you concern, and seek a friend's opinion. (Your mobile phone should double as a camera and torch.)

A compression tester is quite easy to use, and you can screw it into the sparkplug holes of the outer cylinders to check the condition of the cylinders if the vendor agrees. However, it's not so easy to reach the centre cylinder and you may have to leave this. To check cylinder compressions, screw in the compression tester and then kick the bike over with the ignition off (or turn it over on the starter) and the throttle fully open. You should be looking for around 150psi per cylinder on a healthy engine, and with roughly equal readings for each cylinder. Any reading below 125psi shows that the engine is in poor condition. Have a look at the sparkplugs for signs of burnt oil (black and sticky), and check the condition of the sparkplug threads in the head, as they can break up over time with use.

Ideally, have a friend or knowledgeable enthusiast accompany you: a second opinion is always valuable.

# 7 Fifteen minute evaluation
– walk away or stay?

## General condition

Put the bike on its centre stand, to shed equal light on both sides and allow easy access (although putting Triples on their centre stands is not an easy job!) If it's claimed to be restored, and has a nice shiny tank and engine cases, look more closely – how far does the restored finish go? Are the nooks and crannies behind the gearbox and primary chaincase as spotless as the fuel tank? (I once looked at a supposedly restored bike with allegedly vapour blasted crankcases, only to discover that they had in fact been painted with silver paint!) The owner should also have all the receipts as proof of any work completed.

**Engine and frame numbers should match.**

A generally faded look all over isn't necessarily a bad thing – it suggests a machine that hasn't been restored or messed around with, and isn't pretending to be something it is not. Check for any missing parts like side panels, and damage to the exhausts, and look at the condition of the paint and chromework.

Look at the engine – by far the most expensive and time-consuming part of a bike to put right, especially on a Triple. Rebuilt correctly, these engines

**Engines are mechanically noisy, with chatter from the tappets.**

shouldn't leak oil, despite what people might say. There should be no oil on the engine and no drips underneath – get down and have a good look and see how much is there. Remember that oil will always appear to drip from the bottom of the engine, but that isn't necessarily where it's leaking from!

Try the clutch lever. Triple clutches are a little heavy, but not unduly so. A very stiff or jerky lever is a sign that something's not right.

Start the engine (a Triple's centre stand should be strong enough to tolerate this) – it should start within two to three kicks, although the carbs (all three!) will need tickling, and possibly some choke if it's cold. The bike should rev up crisply and cleanly with no blue or black smoke. If it's a T160, check that the electric start works. Triple engines are pretty noisy in terms of tappet rattle round the top end of the engine, so that's nothing to worry about (unless it's really, really loud!), but listen for any rumbles or knocks from the bottom end or the primary chaincase, as these suggest that major work is required. Check that the red oil pressure warning light goes out immediately and doesn't come on again, and that the ammeter, on earlier

Put the bike on its centre stand and have a good, slow walk round it.

The first two letters of the engine number tell you the model year and month of manufacture. This T160 is EK – May '75.

bikes fitted with them, shows charge. Before turning off the engine rev it and check again for blue smoke.

With the engine off, check for play in the forks, headstock and swinging arm. Are there any signs of oil weeping from the front or rear suspension? Are details like the tank, the colour, the side panels, brakes and forks correct for the model year?

## Spotting a fake

Since most variants of the Trident and Rocket III differed only in cycle parts – tank, side panels, forks, wheel hubs and brakes, it's relatively easy to change the identity of a machine by bolting on the relevant bits. Nothing wrong with that, as long as it's made clear that this is the case and the bike isn't being sold as something that it isn't. Original bikes are always worth more than those that are 'mixed and matched.' Engine and frame numbers provide the model year and month of manufacture, and this is a good indication of the bike's authenticity.

Hurricanes and specials are a bit more problematic. Since Hurricanes are

Watch out for cracked or damaged casings.

based on the Rocket III, it is relatively easy to transform a Rocket III into a more valuable Hurricane, and buyers should carry out a thorough check of the provenance of a bike they are buying. That said, Rocket IIIs are quite valuable in their own right, and you need one in order to build a replica Hurricane. The effort involved in this means that there aren't that many fakes around, but as the value of these machines continues to rise so does the possibility of non-genuine Hurricanes appearing.

Specials, especially ex-racing machines and limited editions, are also a problem as they can be readily faked, too. For instance, Les Williams made 28 replicas of the infamous 'Slippery Sam,' but some enthusiasts went on to build their own, and these aren't as valuable. Purchasers of any historic special or racing machine should check the provenance of the bike very carefully before parting with their cash. Note:

What's this? A Rocket III fitted with Hurricane forks, wheels and mudguards – fine if advertised as such.

Replicas of such specials are often great, well-built bikes, but they are naturally worth considerably less than the genuine article. Contact the TR3OC if in doubt.

## Documentation

If the seller claims to be the bike's owner, make sure that they really are by checking the registration document (log book or V5C). Whilst the person listed on the registration document isn't necessarily the bike's owner, their details should match those of the person selling the bike. You can also use the registration document to check engine and frame numbers, and whether the bike has been imported from America.

There may also be old MoT certificates from when Triples required this annual safety check (up to 2018), and these help shed light on the bike's history, especially the mileage. The more, the better – if there are none, why is that?

# 8 Key points
– where to look for problems

Is electronic ignition fitted? The bike will be easier to start, and will run better if so. It's generally another indication of a well-cared for bike.

One of the most important aspects of the bike is the owner. How long have they had the bike? How knowledgeable are they? Do they have a decent range of tools, and are they a member of the TR3OC or TOMCC? A knowledgeable, conscientious owner is one of the surest signs of a good, well-cared for machine.

Check how smooth and heavy the clutch is. If it's very stiff or juddery, there's a problem. Clutch problems can be hard to fix. Check for ease of gear/neutral selection when the engine is running.

Check for blue smoke out of one or both exhausts. This is an indication of bore wear: a common fault with Triples, and hard/expensive to cure.

# 9 Serious evaluation
– 30 minutes for years of enjoyment

Score each section using the boxes as follows: 4 = excellent; 3 = good;
2 = average; 1 = poor. The totting up procedure is detailed at the end of the chapter.
Be realistic in your marking!

## Engine/frame numbers    ▢4  ▢3  ▢2  ▢1

The frame and engine numbers should usually match if the bike is original. The first
two letters of the frame/engine number will tell you the month and production year
of the bike and they use a simple code. The first letter will give you the month of
manufacture and the second the model year. The months don't run sequentially (of
course!), and the 12 letters that represent the 12 months are: A, B, C, D, E, G, H, J,
K, N, P, X. Likewise, the year letters use the same sequence, beginning with C for
1969: C, D, E, G, H, J, K, N. Therefore the frame/engine number for a 1970 model
year bike built in May would begin with 'ED.' The frame/engine number should
also have the model of the bike at the beginning or end of it, eg T150 or A75 (BSA
Rocket III). A bike that doesn't have matching engine and frame numbers is always
worth less.

## Paint    ▢4  ▢3  ▢2  ▢1

There isn't that much paint on a Triple, but what there is makes a big impact.
All Triples have painted tanks and side panels, and earlier models had painted
mudguards as well, with later models having chrome ones.

The paint finish on Triples was generally very good and lasts well. Slightly faded
or worn original paint can be very desirable (patina!), and can add value. Increasingly
more buyers are looking for originality rather than fresh restoration, so paintwork is
very important. On the other hand, a cheap respray can definitely detract from value,
as the tank will have to be properly repainted, which costs money.

If looking at a Hurricane, carefully check the fibreglass tank/seat unit for leaks or
splits. New ones are currently available,
but they aren't cheap or original.

## Chrome    ▢4  ▢3  ▢2  ▢1

There is quite a lot of chrome on a
Triple: wheel rims, fork stanchions,
fork ears, headlamp shells, exhaust
system, handlebars, grab rails, push
rod tubes, and rear shock absorbers,
plus mudguards and indicators on later
models. All this should be checked
carefully, as re-chroming is often
difficult and expensive. If the wheel rims
are rusted, for example, this means

**Rusty chrome wheel rims.**

dismantling and then rebuilding the wheels in order to either re-chrome or replace
the wheel rim – not a simple job.

Fork stanchions are prone to pitting and wearing from age. This causes leaks
from the fork oil seals, although earlier models had rubber gaiters which help reduce

(but not prevent) such damage. As well as small trim items, silencers can rust quite quickly and replacement is often the best solution – but these aren't cheap.

## Tinwork

There isn't too much metal on Triples, but what there is should be in good condition. Tanks should always be inspected for significant rust inside and any signs of poor repair underneath. Oil tank brackets, on the top of the oil tank, are prone to cracking and cause oil leaks. All mudguards are steel, and earlier versions were painted, whilst late ones were chromed. Rear mudguards never really lined up with the rear wheel, so don't worry too much if they're slightly out of line. Side panels (where fitted) were all fibreglass, and these crack rather than rust, so check them for that.

## Badges

There are badges on the sides of most Triples (apart from the Hurricane) and these should be in good condition, as should the badges on the side panels where fitted. Note that the Triumph Trident T160 was to have been called the 'Thunderbird III' and the name was only changed due to concerns over copyright issues with Ford. Early Rocket IIIs were badged as 'Rocket 3,' and later models as 'Rocket Three.'

## Seats

Seats are generally very durable on all Triples, and while they may be a little worn they shouldn't be tatty or ripped. Trident and Rocket III seats hinge open and Hurricane seats lift away completely. The main electrics are revealed under the seat and should be checked carefully (see later section). One item to note is that T150s made for the American market had shorter tanks, so the seat padding was extended on those models to cover the gap between tank and seat – sometimes the incorrect, shorter seat is fitted to these bikes by mistake, leaving a gap between seat and tank.

## Rubbers

Footrest rubbers, gearlever rubber, kickstart rubber and front fork gaiter rubbers (where fitted) are often a good indication of how well the bike has been looked after. Rubbers (especially modern repro ones) can wear quite quickly, and a proud and more meticulous owner will look after them and replace them when necessary – this gives a pointer as to how well the rest of the bike has been maintained. Front fork gaiters may be split, and it's quite a big job to replace them.

Very worn gaiters on an early T150.

## Frames

There were two basic frames for Triples: single down-tube frames for Tridents and a double, cradle frame for Rocket

IIIs. Both frames are very good and shouldn't present any problems in normal use. The only real problems are caused by accident damage. To check for a bent frame look down the side of both wheels to see if they're the same on either side and on a test run check that the bike isn't squirming or pulling hard to one side or the other – both these symptoms are indicative of a bent frame.

You should also check the sidestand mounting, which can crack, especially when owners have been starting the engine with the bike on the sidestand. Apart from this, check the frame number on the left-hand-side of the headstock. It should match the engine number. If the numbers don't match, then the bike may still be good, but it will always be worth less than a matching numbers machine.

Frames on Hurricanes are basically the same as for a Rocket III with the rear loop cut down behind the seat. Frames on T160s were also slightly modified from the earlier T150s.

This T160 has a damaged rear frame loop.

Check for bent frames!

Tridents used single down-tube frames.

BSA opted for the cradle frame with two down tubes.

Check wheel bearings and swinging arm for play.

Check for play in the swinging arm by rocking the rear wheel sideways with the bike on the main stand. There should be no sideways movement. Note that there is a grease nipple fitted to the underside of the swinging arm and it should be greased regularly, so check for signs of this. If it has been left dry the swinging arm bushes can wear or seize.

## Main stands  ④ ③ ② ①

Main stands were very solid on all Triples, and shouldn't give trouble. If there is a problem with the stand, it might signify some other problem with the frame. The only real issue with the centre stands is getting the bike up onto them! They're heavy machines (especially the T160), and it takes quite a bit of effort. Some owners fit lift handles (upside down rear foot pegs) to the rear of the frame to assist.

## Lights  ④ ③ ② ①

Lighting is pretty good on all Triples, with good headlamps and decent rear lights powered by a 12-volt Lucas alternator. The Triumph units are standard Lucas ones of the era whilst the Rocket III/ Hurricane has a smaller, more delicately sculpted tail light.

Tail light on a Rocket III.

## Electrics/wiring ☒4☒ ☒3☒ ☒2☒ ☒1☒

The electrics are pretty standard Lucas fare of the period, with a 12-volt alternator with regulator and Zener diode, triple contact breaker points, and triple ignition coils. Alternators, regulators and Zener diodes do occasionally fail, but most problems are usually associated with poor wiring connections – earlier models used bullet connectors, with the T160 using multi-pin connectors. Replacement and upgraded charging systems are available.

Triples were all originally equipped with points ignition – three of them – and this can be difficult to set up correctly and can even lead to holed pistons, etc. Most bikes have by now been converted to electronic ignition (there are several on the market to choose from). If you want a totally original bike then look for a bike with points, otherwise look for electronic ignition, which is generally superior.

T150 underseat wiring – with electronic ignition box.

## Switchgear ☒4☒ ☒3☒ ☒2☒ ☒1☒

Switchgear changed during production from simple dip switches and horn buttons on the early models through to good quality cast alloy switchgear on later models (which work well, but aren't labelled!) ending with a good quality switchgear on the T160, which was labelled and easier to use. (Note that the horn push doubles as a headlamp flash on the T160 switches). Although rugged, the Bakelite switches themselves can snap off on the

Proper switchgear on a T160. Horn button doubles as a headlamp flasher.

**Early Triple switchgear.**

**Good quality cast alloy switchgear on later Triples – pity they don't give a clue as to which switch does what!**

alloy units, but these are generally available to buy separately as service kits.

## Wheels/tyres

Wheels were fitted with spoked wheels with good quality chrome rims. Check for rust on the rims, as they will have to be dismantled if re-chroming is required. Check the condition of the tyres. As these bikes don't tend to be ridden regularly, the tyres don't wear too fast, so old tyres with cracked sidewalls and dried-out rubber are more likely to be a problem than over-worn treads. There will be a

**The week and year of manufacture is embossed on tyres – this version uses the last four digits to give the date. This tyre looks good, but was in fact made in December (week 51) 2006!**

long number stamped on the tyre wall after the word 'DOT.' The last four digits of this number tell you the week and year of manufacture.

## Wheel hubs/bearings

Early models have a straight hub, and later drum brake models have alloy 'conical hubs.' These later hubs work well but the bearing housing in the rear hubs can wear allowing the bearing to work loose. Check carefully for play in the rear wheel (with the bike on the main stand rock and twist the rear wheel) if there is play it may be just the bearing that's the problem, but it may be a worn hub, and they are NLA. Repairs can be effected however, if necessary. Later models with disc brakes used straight alloy hubs on those wheels fitted with discs.

## Suspension

The basic suspension setup was the same for all Triples with front telescopic forks and twin rear shocks, but the front forks on early models had steel lower fork legs with external springs under a rubber gaiter. Later models used Ceriani forks with alloy lower fork legs, with later models adapted to accept a front disc brake. (Note that twin discs were never fitted to any production Triple, but twin-disc conversions are now available, although they're not cheap!). The main problem with the forks is that, like most forks, they can leak oil where the stanchions enter the lower fork legs. Check for leaks here – misting/oily dirt round the bottom of gaiters on early models is a tell-tale sign. This is often caused by pitting on the chrome of the fork stanchions, so check these carefully if they are exposed. The forks should travel up and down easily and smoothly.

Rear shock absorbers can leak and lose effectiveness. Check for leaks and rust or oil on the central shaft inside the springs. Replacements and upgraded items are readily available.

**Conical rear hub on a T150V.**

**Check fork stanchions for signs of pitting, which can cause oil leaks.**

## Steering head bearings

As with most bikes, the steering head bearings can't be greased in situ so are often ignored, and often over-tightened, which results in a stiff and uneven operation.

With the bike on the centre stand, swing the handlebars from side to side to check for roughness or stiff patches. New bearings are quite cheap, but it's a big job to replace them. To check for play, take the bike off the main stand and rock it backwards and forwards with the front brake on – if there's play you can hear and feel it through the handlebars. In this case it may mean that the bearings simply need re-tightening, but until that's done, you won't know. T160s used taper roller head bearings which are less prone to wear.

## Instruments

All Triples have rev counters (tachos) and speedos fitted as standard. If the needle isn't steady on either instrument it may just be the cable or lack of lubrication inside the gauge. If the gauge does need reconditioning, there are firms that will do this at a price. Early models also had an ammeter fitted, which should show good charge with the lights off, and a little charge with the lights on and the engine above 2000 revs. Note that the red warning light is not an ignition warning light, but an oil pressure one, and this should go out as soon as the bike is started. If it comes on at tickover then it's a sign that the main bearings and/or big end bearings are worn, and a complete engine rebuild will be required in the near future.

Ignition switches, light switches and choke levers changed position at will throughout the production run!

Early T150 instruments with an ammeter.

'71 Rocket III instruments.

Trident '73 T150V instruments with cone-shaped headlamp.

Instrument binnacle on a T160. Chromed by the owner in this case.

## Engine/gearbox – general impressions

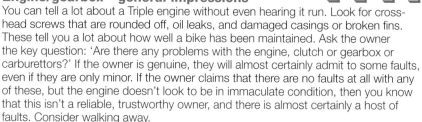

You can tell a lot about a Triple engine without even hearing it run. Look for cross-head screws that are rounded off, oil leaks, and damaged casings or broken fins. These tell you a lot about how well a bike has been maintained. Ask the owner the key question: 'Are there any problems with the engine, clutch or gearbox or carburettors?' If the owner is genuine, they will almost certainly admit to some faults, even if they are only minor. If the owner claims that there are no faults at all with any of these, but the engine doesn't look to be in immaculate condition, then you know that this isn't a reliable, trustworthy owner, and there is almost certainly a host of faults. Consider walking away.

Ask the owner what work they have done or had done to the bike whilst in their ownership (again, if they haven't owned the bike for very long it could be because they discovered faults after they bought it that are too expensive to fix, so they're selling the bike on). Triples, like most contemporary machines, need to be looked after, and regular maintenance, by someone with good mechanical knowledge, is essential.

You should also look into the oil tank (under the seat) to check the oil level and cleanliness, which gives an idea of how recently it was serviced. On the subject of oil, yes, Triples *can* leak, but a really well put together engine, or possibly a very original one that hasn't been messed about with, shouldn't leak oil at all, so don't believe a seller who tells you that 'They all leak oil like that.'

These are some of the more common places for oil to leak from, what they're often caused by, and the remedy:

• The top of the chrome pushrod tubes running up the centres of the cylinder barrels. Cause: poorly fitted or poor quality pushrod gaskets. Remedy: cylinder head removal to enable replacement of pushrod gaskets, and possibly upgrade to alloy pushrod tubes.

Broken cylinder head fins.

Check for oil leaks.

• The rocker box and the tappet covers. Cause: poorly fitted gaskets. Remedy: possibly just new gaskets on the tappet covers (or new 'O' rings on the circular rocker box inspection caps), but just as likely to require rocker box gasket replacement, too, which requires removal of the rocker boxes.

• The cylinder head to cylinder barrel joint. Cause: Triples have oil drain holes from the rocker boxes going down through the head and barrels, which can leak where the head joins the barrels. Remedy: cylinder head removal, possible head skimming and refitting with a new gasket.

• The rear of the primary chaincase. Cause: most likely a failed oil seal between the (wet) primary chain and (dry) clutch, allowing oil into the clutch housing behind the primary chaincase. Oil then drips out of the bottom of the clutch housing through a little air hole. Remedy: strip down primary chaincase and replace oil seal. On early machines this leak may be from the gearbox, not the primary chaincase; see note below.*

• Oil dripping from the sump can suggest that the sump plate gasket is leaking (the sump plate has to be removed to drain the engine oil), and drips from the centre bottom of the primary chaincase can suggest a leaking primary chain gasket. However, as these are both at the bottom of the engine, the oil could be leaking from somewhere else and running down unseen.

*Early engines didn't have a very good seal to the rear of the gearbox, so oil can drip from there on these bikes. They sometimes did this from new, so it's not necessarily a sign of a poorly maintained engine. You can remedy this by fitting a later high gear shaft with an extra oil seal on it, but this involves stripping the gearbox and primary chaincase to do so.*

Ask about and check for 'wet sumping,' where the oil from the oil tank can slowly drain into the sump of the engine if left standing, causing problems when the bike is started. Triple engines do have an anti-drain valve fitted to the oil feed, but these were never very effective. Remove the cap from the oil tank and check the oil level – this gives you an idea as to whether the bike wet sumps or not, but if it has recently been started you won't be able to tell. Aftermarket anti-drain valves can be fitted to the oil tanks to prevent wet sumping, but some owners are concerned that these may restrict oil flow.

Another potential problem to look for with Triples is evidence of a previously broken conrod that has damaged the crank cases. Triples do have a tendency

**Whoops! The timing side conrod made a bid for freedom!**

(though still only rarely) to snap conrods, which in turn leads to severe damage of the crankcases. In such instances crankcases are either mended (where possible) or new cases fitted. Look for signs of major repairs to the crankcases, as severe damage can put the cases out of line.

Likewise, if just one of the three main crankcases has been replaced, the crankshaft may run slightly out of line. However, this is hard to establish during a first viewing. Crankcases were all stamped with the same number (not the engine number) in the factory once they had been line-bored, to show they were a matched set, but the numbers aren't that easy to see.

As for the gearbox, again, check for signs of oil leakage underneath – there shouldn't be any on a good gearbox. Later models (late T150Vs and T160s) have a dipstick to check the gearbox oil level, whilst earlier machines have a level tube accessed from underneath the gearbox, which isn't easy to check.

Can you spot where the centre conrod broke through the crankcase on this T160?

Hurricane with larger cylinder head.

## Engine starting/idling

If in good condition, the engine should start on the first or second kick (or first push of the button for T160s). The procedure is to tickle all three carbs (Triple Amal Concentrics). Tickling the centre carb is difficult, as it's very hard to reach – many owners fit extended ticklers, and the T160 has a special tickle lever, which makes it much easier. All bikes were fitted with chokes (turn the lever anti-clockwise to turn on the chokes; clockwise to turn them off) and the owner should know how much choke their machine requires. Some owners remove the choke slides completely now that bikes aren't often used in the winter, in which case the holes for the choke cables in the top of the carbs should have been blocked off.

Electric start motors aren't the most powerful, but are perfectly capable of starting the engine easily and quickly if they are working properly and have a good (preferably uprated) battery fitted.

Once started, you'll be greeted by that wonderful Triple roar! Don't get too emotional at this – it's easy to be bowled over by the sound of a Triple engine on song, and agree to a purchase no matter what! The engine should soon settle down to an even tickover when warmed up.

At this point check the ammeter (If it's fitted) and the oil pressure warning light, which should not come back on, even at tick over. If fitted (as on Legends) check the oil pressure gauge, which should go straight up to above 90psi with the engine cold.

## Engine smoke/noise

One of the major problems associated with Triple engines is that of burning oil. Some Triples will never burn oil, others tend to do so, no matter what. The reason for this is a problem with the cylinder bores and/or the piston rings. The only way to cure the problem is having the cylinders honed or re-bored and new piston rings (and possibly pistons) fitted, which is an expensive operation. Check the exhaust for blue smoke out of one or both silencers. Black smoke on start-up is quite normal, especially with the choke on, but after that there should not be any blue smoke. Let the engine idle and then blip the throttle; if there's any blue smoke, it's a sure sign there is a problem with the cylinder bores and/or piston rings, requiring major work – and it may still smoke afterwards!

Also bear in mind that Triples often only start smoking when they're hot, so if at all possible, take the bike for a decent test ride and watch in the mirrors for blue smoke on acceleration, and once again blip the throttle after a period of idling on your return. (Also check the oil pressure light remains off with the engine hot.)

Blue smoke on the over-run during deceleration usually means that the valve guides are worn, but this isn't such a common fault, or as difficult to cure.

The top end of a Triple is pretty noisy, so considerable tappet 'chatter' is quite normal, but there should be no knocks or rumbles from the bottom end of the engine, which signifies problems with the big ends or main bearings.

Check that the oil is returning properly in the oil tank (it tends to spit and spurt, which is quite normal).

**The T160 engine looks good – and the starter motor should work without a problem.**

## Primary drive

There shouldn't be any particular noise from the primary chaincase. A knocking sound, especially when pulling away, is symptomatic of worn rubbers in the engine shock absorber (mounted in front of the clutch to the rear of the primary chaincase) and these will need replacing.

You can check the tension and condition of the primary chain by removing the inspection cap and feeling the chain tension with your finger. On T160s it's important to remember that primary chains are NLA, and so if the chain is slack or near the end of its adjustment the only recourse will be to either fit a belt drive or a triplex

A belt drive conversion for a T160, as the original duplex chains are no longer available for this model.

chain conversion – either one is quite expensive. If a belt drive has been fitted, ask how long since it was, as the belts need changing every few years even if not used much.

If fitting a triplex chain conversion to replace the original duplex one on a T160, don't use cheap chains!

## Clutch

One major difference between the Triples and other similar bikes of the era was the clutch. Most machines ran a wet multi-plate clutch (running in oil), whilst the Triples used a single dry plate clutch (similar to most cars). The dry clutch sits between the primary chaincase and the gearbox, and whilst in theory it's a good design, in practice it can be a nightmare.

There are two main problems: the clutch can be heavy to operate, and it can drag – badly. There are several reasons why the clutch doesn't work properly, ranging from something as simple as a rusty or poorly routed clutch cable, through to a distorted clutch pressure plate that requires re-machining. Once set up properly the clutch works well, but this can be far from easy.

Pull in the clutch lever several times. It should be heavy, but not overly so. With the engine running, select first and then see if you can select neutral at standstill. If you can then all is well. If you can't, try engaging neutral on the test run with the bike still moving. If you can, you might possibly get away with minor work on the clutch – but even then an experienced mechanic is often required. If finding neutral is almost impossible at any point, and you can feel the clutch dragging, a complete clutch rebuild by an experienced mechanic may be the only answer.

Note: If you can change gear smoothly on the move, it is almost certainly a clutch problem. However, if the gear change is notchy it could be a gearbox problem.

## Chain/sprockets

With the engine off, check the rear chain and rear sprocket. How clean and well lubricated is the chain? Is it tensioned correctly? (This gives you some idea as to how the rest of the bike has been maintained.) Check for chain wear by lifting the chain away from the rear sprocket: the more you can pull it away, the more worn the chain is. Check the rear sprocket for wear – look at the teeth and check whether they are hooked. If they are, the sprocket needs replacing, and if the rear sprocket needs replacing then the gearbox sprocket almost certainly does, too, and this is a fairly major job. (It is almost impossible to check for wear on the gearbox sprocket without first dismantling the primary chaincase.)

## Battery
Check how old the battery is. More modern replacements are far more powerful and reliable than older types, and a new battery, especially one such as an AGM (Absorbed Glass Mat), is a definite plus; in particular on a T160 or any bike fitted with electric starting.

## Exhaust
Check the condition of the silencers, which shouldn't show signs of rot or corrosion, or dents or scratches. All silencers fitted to Triples were good quality and worked well – even the Black cap silencers (annular discharge silencers) fitted to T160s weren't

**No bluing on these downpipes suggests a well-made aftermarket exhaust system.**

**Check for rusted or damaged silencers.**

restrictive. Owners often blamed them for reducing power on the T160s, but this was due more to the large restrictive air filter fitted to try and reduce emissions. The most efficient silencers of all are actually the Rayguns, which is why so many race bikes had them.

As with most bikes of the era the down pipes can blue quite badly, but some exhaust systems are better than others, so if there's no bluing that's the sign of a good exhaust system and a well-tuned engine.

## Test ride

It's important to take the bike for a test ride (unless it's being sold as a restoration project) as only then can you really assess the condition of the brakes, engine, suspension, clutch, gearbox etc. In order to avoid any awkward situations it is best to discuss this with the seller before arriving to look at the bike. That way everyone is clear about what's happening and you can bring any documents etc. that the seller might ask for before letting you ride the bike (e.g. insurance documents) and what you might leave as assurance that you won't just ride off! (e.g. your vehicle keys or passport etc). If you're going to pay several thousand pounds for a bike you need to check it fully first. If the seller won't allow a test ride, walk away, there's something wrong.

## Engine performance

A Triple engine should pull away strongly without hesitation or misfires, all the way through the rev range. The engine should pull cleanly up to around 5000 revs and then take off like a scalded cat – not that it's recommended to do this on a test run! Check how the engine runs at different throttle openings, from closed right through the rev range. Any hesitation or flat spots means that there's something wrong.

**Triple carburettors can wear out alarmingly quickly. New ones are available.**

From experience this is probably due to the carburettors as they wear out quickly and cause uneven running. Ask the owner about any problems, and if they say 'The carbs just need tuning' it probably means that he's been trying to tune them for ages but has given up – the carbs are worn, so the engine will never run properly. The good news is that new carbs are readily available in standard and 'premier' form at reasonable prices.

## Clutch operation

As mentioned before, this can be a major headache on Triples, so check the clutch operation thoroughly, especially its heaviness and how easy it is to find neutral (T160s have a neutral indicator light, which should work).

## Gearbox operation

Gearboxes should work smoothly and cleanly with little effort required to engage gears. If the gearbox is stiff at standstill it may be the clutch that's the problem; if it's stiff when riding, it's a problem with the gearbox, usually signalling worn selectors and springs. Check that there are no false neutrals between gears, as all gears should select cleanly and easily.

## Handling

Triples generally handle very well (consider that Slippery Sam won the Isle of Man Production TT 5 years in a row!). However, they can be heavy in tight spaces and around town – it's out on the open road that the bike's handling comes into its own. Check that the bike doesn't 'squirm' under you or pull heavily to one side – these are both signs that something is wrong, most probably a bent frame. (Also look at the footrests to see if they are bent upwards – if they are, the bike has probably been dropped at some point in its life.)

## Brakes

Don't expect modern stopping performance from a Triple's brakes. Front Twin Leading Shoe (TLS) drum brakes need to be set up properly, and the shoes can glaze over, whilst the front disc brakes can feel very 'wooden' and aren't that powerful.

Disc brake callipers can also seize or partially seize (adding to the wooden feeling of the brake lever), requiring refurbishment. If the bike is hard to push on the flat, the problem is probably seized callipers.

The good news is that the brakes can be fitted with upgraded callipers and discs, and a twin-disc conversion is also available.

Note that T160s also had rear brake discs rather than drums.

**Early Triple TLS front brake.**

Front drum brake as fitted to later Triples.

Uprated disc brake on this '73 T150V.

**Twin-disc conversion fitted to this T160.**

## Cables

Cables can wear quite quickly, so their condition can give a good idea of how well the bike has been maintained. They should be correctly adjusted and routed (especially the clutch cable – if you can't slide this under the tank slightly, it is probably trapped and making the clutch even stiffer).

Again, the good news is that more modern cable replacements are available, which can make all the difference.

### Evaluation procedure

Add up the total points.

Score: 128 = excellent; 96 = good; 64 = average; 32 = poor. Bikes scoring over 90 will be completely usable and will require only maintenance and care to preserve condition. Bikes scoring between 32 and 65 will require some serious work (at much the same cost regardless of score). Bikes scoring between 66 and 89 will require very careful assessment of the necessary repair/restoration costs in order to arrive at a realistic value.

# 10 Auctions
– sold! Another way to buy your dream

## Auction pros & cons
Pros: Prices will usually be lower than those of dealers or private sellers and you might grab a real bargain on the day. Auctioneers have usually established ownership with the seller. At the venue you can usually examine documentation relating to the vehicle.
Cons: You have to rely on a sketchy catalogue description of condition and history. The opportunity to inspect is limited and you cannot ride the bike – or even start the engine. Auction bikes are often a little below par and may require some work. It's easy to overbid. There will usually be a buyer's premium to pay in addition to the auction hammer price.

## Which auction?
Auctions by established auctioneers are advertised in bike magazines and on the auction houses' websites. A catalogue, or a simple printed list of the lots for auctions might only be available a day or two ahead, though often lots are listed and pictured on auctioneers' websites much earlier. Contact the auction company to ask if previous auction selling prices are available as this is useful information (details of past sales are often available on websites).

## Catalogue, entry fee and payment details
When you purchase the catalogue of the vehicles in the auction, it often acts as a ticket allowing two people to attend the viewing days and the auction. Catalogue details tend to be comparatively brief, but will include information such as 'one owner from new, low mileage, full service history,' etc. It also usually shows a guide price to give you some idea of what to expect to pay, and tells you what is charged as a 'Buyer's premium.' The catalogue also contains details of acceptable forms of payment. At the fall of the hammer an immediate deposit is usually required, the balance payable within 24 hours. If the plan is to pay by cash, there may be a cash limit. Some auctions accept payment by debit card. Sometimes credit or charge cards are acceptable, but they often incur an extra charge. A bank draft or bank transfer will have to be arranged in advance with your own bank as well as with the auction house. No bike will be released before all payments are cleared. If delays occur in payment transfers then storage costs can accrue.

## Buyer's premium
A buyer's premium will be added to the hammer price: don't forget this in your calculations. It is not usual for there to be a further state tax or local tax on the purchase price and/or on the buyer's premium.

## Viewing
In some instances it's possible to view on the day, or days before, as well as in the hours prior to, the auction. While the officials may start the engine for you, a test drive is out of the question. You can also ask to see any documentation available.

## Bidding

Before you take part in the auction, decide your maximum bid – and stick to it! It may take a while for the auctioneer to reach the lot you are interested in, so use that time to observe how other bidders behave. When it's the turn of your bike, attract the auctioneer's attention and make an early bid. The auctioneer will then look to you for a reaction every time another bid is made, usually the bids will be in fixed increments until the bidding slows, when smaller increments will often be accepted before the hammer falls. If you want to withdraw from the bidding, make sure the auctioneer understands your intentions – a vigorous shake of the head when he or she looks to you for the next bid should do the trick!

Assuming that you are the successful bidder, the auctioneer will note your card or paddle number, and from that moment on you will be responsible for the vehicle.

If the bike is unsold, either because it failed to reach the reserve or because there was little interest, it may be possible to negotiate with the owner, via the auctioneers, after the sale is over.

## Successful bid

There are two more items to think about: how to get the bike home, and insurance. If you can't ride the bke, your own or a hired trailer is one way, another is to have the vehicle shipped using the facilities of a local company. The auction house will also have details of companies specialising in the transfer of bikes.

Insurance for immediate cover can usually be purchased on site, but it may be more cost-effective to make arrangements with your own insurance company in advance, and then call to confirm the full details.

## eBay & other online auctions

eBay & other online auctions could land you a bike at a bargain price, though you'd be foolhardy to bid without examining the vehicle first, something most vendors encourage. Another advantage of eBay is that you can view bikes for sale at your convenience via any device connected to the internet. A useful feature of eBay is that the geographical location of the bike is shown, so you can narrow your choices to those within a realistic radius of home. You can also 'watch' different bikes on sale and see how much they eventually sell for. The main thing to remember is that photos can be very misleading, and a rough bike can look just as good as a concours one. Ask for close-up photos, and most definitely see the bike in person before committing yourself to buy. If you do decide to bid, then be prepared to be outbid in the last few moments of the auction. Remember, your bid is binding and that it will be very, very difficult to get restitution in the case of a crooked vendor fleecing you – caveat emptor!

Be aware that some vehicles offered for sale in online auctions are 'ghost' bikes. Don't part with any cash without being sure that the vehicle does actually exist and is as described (usually pre-bidding inspection is possible).

## Auctioneers

**Barrett-Jackson** www.barrett-jackson.com; **Bonhams** www.bonhams.com; **British Car Auctions (BCA)** www.bca-europe.com or www.british-car-auctions.co.uk; **Christies** www.christies.com; **Coys** www.coys.co.uk; **eBay** www.eBay.com or www.eBay.co.uk; **H&H** www.handh.co.uk; **RM Sotheby's** www.rmsothebys.com; **Shannons** www.shannons.com.au; **Silver** www.silverauctions.com

# 11 Paperwork
– correct documentation is essential!

## The paper trail
Classic bikes usually come with a large portfolio of paperwork accumulated and passed on by a succession of proud owners. This documentation represents the real history of the bike, and from it can be deduced the level of care the bike has received, how much it's been used, which specialists have worked on it and the dates of any major repairs and restorations. All of this information will be priceless to you as the new owner, so be very wary of machines with little paperwork to support their claimed history.

## Registration documents
All countries have some form of registration for private vehicles whether it's like the American 'pink slip' system or the British 'log book' system.

It is essential to check that the registration document is genuine, that it relates to the bike in question, and that all the vehicle's details are correctly recorded, including frame and engine numbers. If you are buying from the previous owner, his or her name and address will be recorded in the document: this will not be the case if you are buying from a dealer.

In the UK the current registration document is named 'V5C,' and is printed in coloured sections of blue, green and pink. The blue section relates to the bike's specification, the green section has details of the new owner, and the pink section is sent to the DVLA in the UK when the bike is sold. A small section in yellow deals with selling the bike within the motor trade.

In the UK, the DVLA provides details of earlier keepers of the vehicle upon payment of a small fee, and much can be learned in this way.

If you are importing a bike from abroad, the main document to have is the NOVA certificate (Notification of Vehicle Arrival), which means that all the relevant import duties and taxes have been paid. With this, registering the bike in the UK is quite straightforward, if a little bureaucratic. As well as the NOVA, you need to insure it (on the frame number), have the bike authenticated by the owners' club (TR3OC), provide the receipt of purchase, and complete a rather onerous form and send it all off to the DVLA. Without the NOVA document it can be a complete nightmare. Note that to register a Triple in the UK you no longer require an MoT, which is great news as it means you can register a restoration project as soon as you get it and not have to wait until it's restored and MoT'd before you can apply.

## Roadworthiness certificate (MoT)
In the UK it is no longer a requirement to have an MoT on any vehicle over 40 years old, so this includes all Triples; although, some owners choose to still MoT their bikes every year. Whatever the case, a good owner should have all the past certificates from when the bike did require an MoT (up to May 2018), and these show mileage and give a good idea of how the bike has been used.

It can be a good idea to ask that the bike is given an MoT as part of the deal, just for peace of mind. I think this depends on how mechanically minded you are. If you're not, and don't trust your own checks, then an MoT might be a good idea. But just remember that an MoT doesn't cover any part of the engine or gearbox.

## Road licence

Road tax for all vehicles built over 40 years ago is free, and that includes all Triples! So, generally good news: no MoT and no road tax. However, speaking as an eternal pessimist, I wonder when restrictions might start being placed on 'Historic Vehicles' in the future, on environmental grounds: 'Can only be ridden at the weekend,' 'Can't be ridden in town centres,' etc. But, hey, let's enjoy things while we still can!

## Certificates of authenticity

It is possible to get a certificate proving the age and authenticity of a bike (eg engine and frame numbers, and paint colour) of a particular vehicle. These are sometimes called 'Heritage Certificates' and if the bike comes with one of these it is a definite bonus. If you want to obtain one, then contact the TR3OC.

## Valuation certificate

Hopefully, the vendor will have a recent valuation certificate, or letter signed by a recognised expert stating how much he, or she, believes the particular bike to be worth (such documents, together with photos, are usually needed to get 'agreed value' insurance). Generally such documents should act only as confirmation of your own assessment of the bike rather than a guarantee of value: some owners can exaggerate the value of their bikes on their insurance, others minimise it in order to reduce premiums.

## Service history

Often these bikes will have been serviced at home by enthusiastic (and hopefully capable) owners for a good number of years. Nevertheless, try to obtain as much service history and other paperwork pertaining to the bike as you can. Naturally specialist garage receipts score most points in the value stakes. However, anything helps in the great authenticity game, items like the original bill of sale, handbook, parts invoices and repair bills; anything that adds to the story and the character of the bike. Even a brochure correct to the year of the bike's manufacture is a useful document and something that you could well have to search hard to locate in future years.

If the seller claims to have carried out regular servicing, ask what work was completed, when, and seek some evidence of it being carried out. Your assessment of the bike's overall condition should tell you whether the seller's claims are genuine.

## Restoration photographs and receipts

If the seller tells you that the bike has been restored, then expect to be shown a series of photographs taken while the restoration was under way. Pictures taken at various stages, and from various angles, should help you gauge the thoroughness of the work. If you buy the bike, ask if you can have all the photographs as they form an important part of the vehicle's history. Along with any photographic records you should also check all the receipts for any work that the owner has claimed to have had done. These should be comprehensive. If any are missing, then at best the owner is disorganised and at worst they are untruthful. (I once bought a bike with a supposedly fully rebuilt engine for which the seller had 'lost' the receipts. I later discovered that the engine had never been rebuilt at all.)

# 12 What's it worth?
– let your head rule your heart

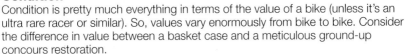

## Condition

Condition is pretty much everything in terms of the value of a bike (unless it's an ultra rare racer or similar). So, values vary enormously from bike to bike. Consider the difference in value between a basket case and a meticulous ground-up concours restoration.

An evaluation of the bike should enable you to consider whether its condition is excellent/concours, good, average, poor or basket case, and this will give some indication of the bike's value.

Before looking at a bike, check the prices that other vendors are asking – and whether or not they made a sale! eBay is always a good starting point, as it is free and instant, and you can 'watch' an item and find out how much it finally sells for (if it does). However, remember the golden rule: photos on eBay may make a bike appear to be in better condition than it really is (the photo of a concours bike will look similar to a photo of a bike in average condition). Apart from that, you should look at bikes for sale in different classic motorcycle magazines, as well as checking the results of motorcycle auctions.

Remember that bikes sold by a dealer are always more expensive than those sold privately, and bikes sold at auction are generally cheaper (although not always!).

Prices are currently very strong for Triples in general. Hurricane X-75 prices have recently gone through the roof, and T160 prices remain very strong, as do most Rocket III prices, due to the model's relative rarity. T150 values continue to rise as well. The value of genuine works racers and other exotica is still very high, and specials such as the Hyde Harrier are always highly sought after. Very early bikes in original condition are also increasingly valued, and command considerably higher prices.

However, when it comes to values we also ought to consider how future environmental legislation might affect classic vehicles and their monetary worth. Will legislation be brought in to restrict the use of 'Historic Vehicles,' banning them from town centres or from everyday use, etc? Whatever the case, restrictions are on the horizon, and in the very long-term it will become increasingly difficult to buy fresh petrol as most vehicles become electric. So, what effect might this have on the value of classic vehicles, including BSA/Triumph Triples? No-one really knows, but it is something that any prospective purchaser should bear in mind.

Before making an offer, consider whether this is the bike for you? Is it the model and condition you were looking for, and has it been modified? If modified, do you like or want the modifications? If you don't then you'll simply be paying twice – once for the upgrade, and then again to revert to the original. Is the seller genuine? Is the bike genuine? How does the asking price compare with that of similar bikes on sale?

Negotiate on the basis of your assessment of the bike and its seller. Be realistic about value, and be ready for at least some flexibility – a small increase in your offer can often clinch the deal.

# 13 Do you really want to restore?

– it'll take longer and cost more than you think

Many owners like to do some work on their bikes, even at a basic level, and it's worth noting that whatever Triple you buy it will always require some form of ongoing maintenance, no matter what. The question is, how much mechanical work do you want to get involved in?

**Rebuilding a Triple engine can be very rewarding.**

If you are considering restoring a bike from scratch, but you haven't done so before, you might consider restoring something like a Triumph Bonneville first, as they are that bit more straightforward to work on. Don't be put off from restoring a Triple, but just be aware that they're that little bit more difficult to get right – but when they are right, they're wonderful!

Restoration takes time, money, space, and at least some degree of mechanical ability, but it can be very rewarding, plus you get to learn and understand so much more about the bike you are riding. For those who do decide to go down this route there are various helpful manuals, not least *The Triumph Trident and Rocket III Restoration Manual*, written by yours truly – highly recommended! But do not underestimate the amount of time and money it takes to complete a full ground-up restoration.

As I say, though, there'll always be jobs that need carrying out on any Triple, so you won't completely miss out on all the mechanical fun if you decide not to restore it yourself.

An alternative is to have the bike professionally restored. Be aware, however, that this can be very expensive due to the sheer amount of labour involved in such an undertaking – and then you've got the cost of all the parts, etc, on top of that. Also, a professional restoration can take a very long time, as professional outfits tend to be quite small operations, and there may be a long waiting list.

If you are considering a full restoration or major engine work by someone else, I suggest contacting one of the recommended specialists listed in the back of this book.

Another alternative is to complete a 'rolling restoration' where the bike is on the road and some work is done now and then, rather than the bike being completely out of use. This is a possibility for bikes in generally fair to good condition. One advantage is that a lot of work can be carried out over winter with the bike still available to ride during the summer. The main problem is that until a rolling restoration is complete, the bike will never be right, and therefore you won't enjoy riding it that much, and this might continue for some time. Also, you tend to lose impetus/momentum over time, and the next planned part of the restoration never happens.

Whatever the case, it's a big part of choosing which machine to buy.

**This restoration project isn't for the faint-hearted!**

# 14 Paint problems
– bad complexion, including dimples, pimples and bubbles

Paint faults generally occur due to accidental damage, a lack of protection/ maintenance, or poor preparation prior to a respray or touch-up. Some of the following conditions may be present in the bike you're looking at.

## Orange peel

This appears as an uneven paint surface, similar to the appearance of the skin of an orange. The fault is caused by the failure of atomized paint droplets to flow into each other when they hit the surface. It's sometimes possible to rub out the effect with proprietary paint cutting/rubbing compound or very fine grades of abrasive paper. A respray may be necessary in severe cases. Consult a bodywork repairer/paint shop for advice on the particular tank or panel.

## Cracking

Severe cases are likely to have been caused by too heavy an application of paint (or filler beneath the paint). Also, insufficient stirring of the paint before application can lead to the components being improperly mixed, and cracking can result. Incompatibility with the paint already on the panel can have a similar effect. To rectify the problem, it is necessary to rub down to a smooth, sound finish before respraying the problem area.

## Crazing

Sometimes when the problems mentioned under 'Cracking' are present, the paint takes on a crazed rather than a cracked appearance. This problem can also be caused by a reaction between the underlying surface and the paint. Paint removal and respraying the problem area is usually the only solution.

A high quality paint job on this Rocket III tank.

Chipped paint.

Dented petrol tank.

## Blistering

Almost always caused by corrosion of the metal beneath the paint. Usually perforation is found in the metal and the damage is usually worse than that suggested by the area of blistering. The metal will have to be repaired before repainting.

## Micro blistering

Usually the result of an economy respray, where inadequate heating has allowed moisture to settle on the tank before spraying. Consult a paint specialist, but usually damaged paint will have to be removed before partial or full respraying.

## Fading

Some colours, especially reds, are prone to fading if subjected to strong sunlight for long periods without the benefit of polish protection. Sometimes proprietary paint restorers and/or paint cutting/rubbing compounds will retrieve the situation. Often a respray is the only real solution.

Fading paint.

Tank in better condition than it looks.

## Peeling

Often a problem with metallic paintwork when the sealing lacquer becomes damaged and begins to peel off. Poorly applied paint may also peel. The remedy is to strip and start again!

## Dimples

Dimples in the paintwork are caused by the residue of polish (particularly silicone types) not being removed properly before respraying. Paint removal and repainting is the only solution.

# 15 Problems due to lack of use

– just like their owners, Tridents/Rocket IIIs need exercise

Like any piece of engineering, Triples deteriorate if they sit doing nothing for long periods. This is especially the case if the bike is laid up for six months of the year, as some classics are.

## Rust

If the bike is put away wet, or worse, stored in a cold, damp garage, the paint, metal and brightwork will suffer. Ensure the bike is completely clean and dry before it goes into storage, and cover it with a proprietary protective spray, which can be washed off in the spring. Alternatively, buy a good dehumidifier (although they won't work when it's really cold) or a special bike storage bag.

Brake callipers can seize, and brake fluid absorbs water.

## Seized components

Pistons in callipers, slave and master cylinders can seize.

The clutch may seize if the plate becomes stuck to the clutch basket because of corrosion – although, unless severe, this can usually be released by heat from running the engine.

Carburettors can become gummed up with fuel during a long lay-up.

## Fluids

Old, acidic oil can corrode bearings. Brake fluid absorbs water from the atmosphere, and should be renewed every two years. Old fluid with a high water content can cause corrosion and pistons/calipers to seize and can cause brake failure when the water turns to vapour near hot braking components.

Damp storage causes silencers to rust internally.

## Tyre problems

Tyres that have borne the weight of the bike in a single position for some time will develop flat spots, resulting in some vibration. To avoid this, over-inflate the tyres or preferably leave the bike on its centre stand.

The tyre walls may have cracks or (blister type) bulges, meaning new tyres are needed even if the tread is good.

Tyres deteriorate over time.

## Electrics
If the battery is the old lead/acid type, connect it to a battery condition maintainer when leaving it for any length of time. Newer batteries such as the AGM (gel) ones are more tolerant of being left standing, and don't require such maintenance. Wiring connections that water has entered will corrode, so may need spraying with WD40.

## Rotting exhaust system
Exhaust gas contains a high water content, so exhaust systems corrode very quickly from the inside when the bike is not used, especially if stored somewhere damp. Not an easy one to address, but just to be aware of.

## Engine
Old oil is not good for engines and the oil should be changed in the autumn before the bike is put into storage, not in the spring. It is good to turn the engine over occasionally on the kickstart when in storage to lubricate all parts – don't start the engine though as this creates moisture inside the engine which won't burn off as the engine won't be hot enough and corrosion will begin.

Also be aware of the engine wet-sumping, which requires removal of the sump plate, and in turn usually the exhaust, too, in order to drain out the oil. (There is no engine oil drain plug on a Triple, and the only way to drain oil from the sump is to remove the sump plate – unless a modified sump plate with integral drain plug has been fitted.)

## Carburettors
As a result of its ethanol content, modern fuel can go off quite quickly and turn into a gooey mess – inside the carburettors! If this happens, remove and thoroughly clean the carbs. Additives are available to add to the tank before a long lay-up, to help prevent this.

# 16 The Community

– key people, organisations and companies in the Trident/Rocket world

## Clubs

Triumph and Rocket Three Owners' Club (TR3OC)
www.tr3oc.com

Triumph Motorcycle Owners' Club (TOMCC)
www.tomcc.org

BSA Owners' Club
www.bsaownersclub.co.uk

BSA Owners' Club of New South Wales
www.bsansw.org.au

New Zealand BSA Motorcycle Owners' Club
www.bsa.org.nz

## Parts and services

LP Williams
Unit 3, South Barn,
Low West End, Claughton,
Nr Lancaster, LA2 9JX
Tel: 01524 770956
www.triumph-spares.co.uk
(Triple spares)

Norman Hyde Classics Ltd
Rigby Close,
Heathcote,
Warwick,
CV34 6TL
Tel: 01926 832345
www.normanhyde.co.uk
(Triple spares and upgrades)

Triple Cycles
Phil Pick,
London
www.triples.co.uk
(Triple spares)

A Gagg & Sons
Unit C21A, Byron Industrial Estate,
Brookfield Rd, Arnold,
Nottingham, NG5 7ER
Tel: 0115 978 6288
www.gaggs.eu
(Instrument repairers)

Burlen Fuel Systems Ltd
Spitfire House, Castle Rd,
Salisbury, Wiltshire,
SP1 3SA
Tel: 01722 412500
www.burlen.co.uk
(Suppliers of Amal carburettors)

Namrick Ltd
The Nut and Bolt Store,
124 Portland Rd,
Hove, East Sussex,
BN3 5QL
Tel: 01273 779864
www.namrick.co.uk
(Suppliers of stainless steel fixings)

Central Wheel Components Ltd
8 & 9, Station Rd, Coleshill,
Birmingham,
B46 1HT
Tel: 01675 462264
www.central-wheel.co.uk
(Specialist wheel building services)

Autosparks
80-88 Derby Rd,
Sandiacre,
Nottingham,
NG10 5HU
Tel: 0115 949 7211
www.autosparks.co.uk
(Suppliers of electrical components)

Prestige Electro Plating,
Unit 6, Cliff St Industrial Estate,
Mexborough,
S64 9HU
Tel: 01709 577004
(Chrome plating and metal polishing
services)

Frost Auto Restoration Techniques Ltd
Crawford St,
Rochdale,
OL16 5NU
Tel: 01706 658619
www.frost.co.uk
(Suppliers of general restoration
equipment)

Triples Rule
www.triplesrule.com
(Suppliers of upgraded parts for Triples)

Triples Unlimited
www.triplesunlimited.com
(Upgraded parts and specialist services
for triples)

Molnar Precision Ltd
Preston,
PR2 0HG
Tel: 01772 700700
www.manx.co.uk
(Suppliers of stainless fittings for Triples)

Clive Scarfe
132 Waveney Drive,
Lowestoft,
Suffolk,
NR33 0TR
Tel: 01502 583915
CliveScarfe@hotmail.com
www.clivescarfesystems.co.uk
(Suppliers of custom stainless
steel parts and T160 primary chain
conversions)

Viking Exhausts
Paul Bryant,
New Zealand
www.vikingexhaust.com
(Suppliers of high quality exhaust
systems)

Dave Madigan
Mad-components,
USA
madigan_analytical_design@yahoo.com
(Suppliers of uprated starter motors and
other custom parts)

Paul Fields
paulrocket3@gmail.com
(Supplier of alloy end caps and stainless
covers for Dave Madigan starter motors,
and twin-disc conversions)

Andy Preece
andypreece5@gmail.com
(Supplier of primary chain locking tools
to facilitate removal of the engine and
shock absorber nuts)

David Drew
David@testvalley.org.uk
(Supplier of special parts including
uprated gearbox plunger and silicone
rubber gaskets)

## Specialists
3D Motorcycles
Richard Darby,
Wolverhampton
www.3Dmotorcycles.eu
(Specialist Triple mechanic)

Rustler Racing Ltd
Martin Russell,
Birmingham
Tel: 0121 784 8266
(Specialist Triple mechanic and frame
expert)

Rob North Triples
Les & Denise Whiston,
West Midlands
www.robnorthtriples.com
(Specialist Triple mechanics and
suppliers of various upgrades, including
electric start conversions)

Triple Tecs
Trident & Rocket III racing and
restoration services,
California
www.tripletecs.com
(Specialist Triple mechanics)

P&M Motorcycles
Brentford, Middlesex,
TW8 9HF
Tel: 02088471711
(Specialist Triple mechanics and
suppliers of various upgrades, including
electric start conversion)

Middle England Motorcycles
Clive Blake,
Kent/Sussex
email: triumphtriples@cliveblake.plus.
com
Tel: 07802965092
(Specialist Triple mechanic)

## Publications
*How to Restore the Triumph Trident
T150/T160 & BSA Rocket III* by Chris
Rooke
ISBN: 978-1-845848-82-8

*Triumph and BSA Triples – The
complete story* by Mick Duckworth
ISBN: 1-86126-705-3

*BSA & Triumph Triples Gold Portfolio*
Compiled by R M Clarke (Collected
articles)
ISBN: 1-85520-464-9

*Superbikes and the '70s* by Dave
Sheehan
ISBN: 978-1-909213-12-8

*Triumph Trident and BSA Rocket III
Workshop Manual*, published by Haynes
Publishing.

Other recommended publications
are the Triumph and BSA Workshop
manuals (available to download) and the
Parts Catalogues for different models.
There are also the Service Notes,
compiled and available from the TR3OC.

## Internet
There are several Facebook pages
dedicated to supporting and celebrating
Triples. Here are some of the main ones:
• TR3OC
• The Triumph Trident T150 Owners
  Group
• The Triumph Trident T160
  Appreciation Society
• Triumph Trident Restoration Manual
  Updates
• Bring back the BSA Rocket III

There is also an online forum
dedicated to helping owners
with queries about their bikes:
www.triplesonline.com

# 17 Vital statistics
– essential data at your fingertips

Listing the vital statistics of every model produced would take more room than we have here, so we've chosen the three main models: 1969 BSA Rocket III, 1973 Triumph Trident T150V, and 1975 Triumph Trident T160.

## Max speed
- '69 BSA Rocket III: 127mph
- '73 Triumph Trident T150: 127mph
- '75 Triumph Trident T160: 120mph

## Engine
- '69 BSA Rocket III MkI: Air-cooled overhead valve in-line three slanted cylinders, 741cc. Triple Amal concentric 27mm carburettors. Bore and stroke 67mm x 70mm. Compression ratio 9.5:1. BHP 58bhp @ 7250rpm.
- '73 Triumph Trident T150V: Air-cooled overhead valve in-line three vertical cylinders, 741cc. Triple Amal concentric 27mm carburettors. Bore and stroke 67mm x 70mm. Compression ratio 9.5:1. BHP 58bhp @ 7250rpm.
- '75 Triumph Trident T160: Air-cooled overhead valve in-line three slanted cylinders, 741cc. Triple Amal concentric 27mm carburettors. Bore and stroke 67mm x 70mm. Compression ratio 9.5:1. BHP 58bhp @ 7250rpm.

## Gearbox
- '69 BSA Rocket III MkI: Four-speed. Ratios: First: 11.95:1, Second: 8.3:1, Third: 5.83:1, Fourth: 4.87:1
- '73 Triumph Trident T150V: Five-speed. Ratios: First: 13.59:1, Second: 9.66:1, Third: 7.36:1, Fourth: 6.26:1, Fifth: 5.26:1
- '75 Triumph Trident T160: Five-speed. Ratios: First: 12.71:1, Second: 9.04:1, Third: 6.89:1, Fourth: 5.85:1, Fifth: 4.92:1

## Brakes
- '69 BSA Rocket III MkI: Cable, 8in twin leading shoe front drum, 7in rear drum
- '73 Triumph Trident T150V: Front hydraulic 10in disc, rear 7in drum, conical hub
- '75 Triumph Trident T160: Front hydraulic 10in disc, rear hydraulic 10in disc

## Electrics
- '69 BSA Rocket III MkI: 12-volt, alternator
- '73 Triumph Trident T150V: 12-volt, alternator
- '75 Triumph Trident T160: 12-volt, alternator

## Weight
- '69 BSA Rocket III MkI: 470lb
- '73 Triumph Trident T150V: 468lb
- '75 Triumph Trident T160: 552lb

## Major change points by year
- 1968 Triumph Trident T150 and BSA Rocket III enter production.

- 1970 Trident 'Beauty Kit' launched with re-styled 'classic' tank, side panels and Bonneville style seat, new exhaust system, new mudguards.
- 1971 new telescopic alloy forks, indicators, revised switchgear, new front brake, conical hubs, optional five-speed gearbox, American specification tank available.
- 1972 Triumph Trident T150V: five-speed gearbox standard, front disc brake. BSA Rocket III: five-speed gearbox available on some bikes. BSA Rocket III ceases production.
- 1973 Triumph Hurricane X-75 launched.
- 1975 Triumph Trident T160 launched. Electric start, slanted cylinders, front and rear disc brakes, revised 'classic' styling.
- 1976 Trident ceases production.

**A Harrier pulls a wheelie at Beezumph.**

**Glorious MkI Rocket III.**

**Rocket III with a difference!**

**The Quadrant: a four-cylinder prototype.**

# The Essential Buyer's Guide™ series ...

# ... don't buy a vehicle until you've read one of these!

**Also from Veloce –**

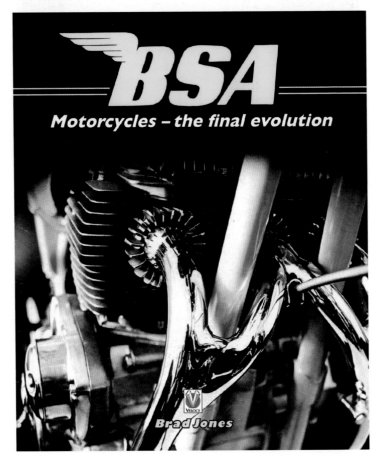

A fresh, much needed appraisal of BSA and Triumph motorcycles designed for the 1971 model year, plus BSA's revolutionary Ariel 3 moped, and the 750cc Triumph Hurricane that was originally planned as a BSA model. This book also presents a comprehensive study of the related promotional and racing events, as well as the US organisation, and an in-depth account of BSA's financial position before and after mid-1971's devastating trading loss announcement.

ISBN: 978-1-845846-47-3
Hardback • 25x20.7cm • 144 pages • 259 colour and b&w pictures

For more information and price details, visit our website at www.veloce.co.uk
• email: info@veloce.co.uk • Tel: +44(0)1305 260068

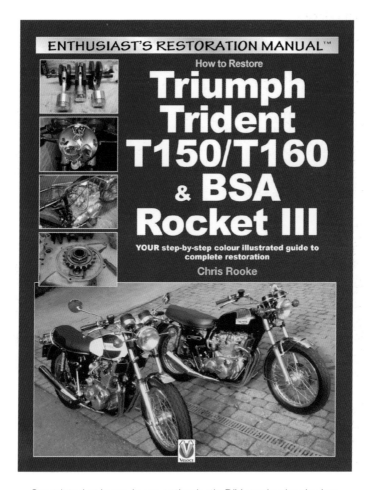

Completed at home by an enthusiastic DIY mechanic who has great experience rebuilding bikes, this book covers the complete restoration of a Triumph Trident T150V and a Triumph T160. Each and every aspect of the dismantling, refurbishment and reassembly of these classic bikes is covered in great detail, accompanied by a host of clear colour photos.

ISBN: 978-1-845848-82-8
Paperback • 27x20.7cm • 232 pages • 704 colour pictures

For more information and price details, visit our website at www.veloce.co.uk
• email: info@veloce.co.uk • Tel: +44(0)1305 260068

# Index

Alternative bikes  7

Battery  39
Beauty Kit  15, 59
Beezumph  9
Bonneville  3, 11, 49
Brakes  9, 41-43, 53

Cables  43
Carburettors  40, 41, 54
Cardinal  17
Chain  38, 39
Chrome  26
Clutch  10, 22, 25, 38, 41
Condition  48

eBay  45, 48
Electric start  6, 10
Electrics/switchgear  30, 31, 33, 54
Electronic ignition  25
Engine/frame numbers  22, 26
Engine/gearbox  34-38, 40, 41, 54
Exhaust  39, 54

Fakes  23, 24
Frames  27-29

Handling  41
History  47
Hurricane  13, 14, 16, 48, 59
Hyde Harrier  17

Importing  46

Legend  17
Lights  29

Norton  3, 11

Ogle  14
Oil pressure  22

Paint  26, 50-52
Primary drive  37, 38

Restoration  49, 50
Rocket III  13, 15, 48, 58, 59
Rust  26, 31, 53

Seats  6, 27
Slippery Sam  11, 17
Smoke  25, 37
Spares  8
Steering  32
Suspension  32
Swinging arm  29

T150  12-15, 48, 58, 59
T160  13, 16, 17, 48, 58, 59

Weights  6
Wheels and tyres  31, 53, 54